P9-AOO-578

SON OF THE SEA.

AN INTRODUCTION TO CHUNG-HUA AND KIRI-E

J. A. CHRISTENSEN

WATSON-GUPTILL
PUBLICATIONS
NEW YORK

To Kumiko-san,
who started it all.

Edited by Marian Appellof
Designed by Bob Fillie
Graphic production by Ellen Greene
Text set in Tiepolo Book

First published in 1989 in New York by Watson-Guptill Publications,
a division of Billboard Publications, Inc.,
1515 Broadway, New York, N.Y. 10036

Library of Congress Cataloging-in-Publication Data

Christensen, J. A. (Jack Arden), 1927–
Cut-art : an introduction to Chung-hua and Kiri-e / J. A.
Christensen.
p. cm.
Bibliography : p.
Includes index.
ISBN 0-8230-1144-5
1. Paper work—China. 2. Paper work—Japan. I. Title.
TT870.C495 1989
736'.98—dc 19 88-38845
CIP

Distributed in the United Kingdom by Phaidon Press Ltd.,
Musterlin House, Jordan Hill Road, Oxford OX2 8DP

Manufactured in Japan

First printing, 1989

1 2 3 4 5 6 7 8 9 10/93 92 91 90 89

ACKNOWLEDGMENTS

As to my own cutting, I would be most remiss if I did not acknowledge, with a note of sincerest appreciation, those many individuals who have helped me in so many ways—so, my deep-felt thanks to Kumiko Kanai, who introduced me to *kiri-e*; to Hatsue Shigetomi, who sent materials and information from Japan that I would otherwise not have been able to obtain; to Reverend Shokai Kanai, who translated information from Japanese for me; to Neal Ivie, who acted as my daily "sounding board" and critic; to Jewel Bindrup, who made the first public exhibition of my work possible; to Ardith Arnberg, who created the first commercial outlet for my work; and to my many friends—especially Marcia Whipps, Betty Ackerlind, Barbara Woll, Robin Lowell, and Bertel Arnberg—who have given me so much encouragement through the years. Sincere appreciation and thanks must also be extended to Executive Editor Mary Suffudy, Associate Editor Marian Appellof, and designer Bob Fillie at Watson-Guptill Publications, whose energy and enthusiasm in behalf of this work have brought a dream into reality.

J. A. CHRISTENSEN
Salt Lake City, Utah

BUTTERFLIES & LILIES.

Contents

Introduction

I WAS IN ABOUT the fifth year of my study of the Japanese Tea Ceremony when this all began. After finishing our weekly lesson, my teacher Kumiko-san and I were involved in a discussion of Japanese art and culture (as we often were) when she suddenly rose and left the room. A few moments later she returned and handed me a couple of pictures that she had evidently clipped from some Japanese magazine.

"Have you ever seen anything like this before?" she asked.

Indeed, I never had. In one picture, two Japanese children stood in a row of corn, the boy wearing a corn-tassel mustache much to the amusement of his companion, who carried a basket filled with ears of corn. In the other picture, a little boy and girl and their pet goat stood in a grove of birch trees waving good-bye to two older children. The designs were delightful; the colors fairly glowed on the page.

"What is it?" I asked.

"*Kiri-e*," she answered.

"Cut-art?"

"Yes. Paper-cuts."

These were paper-cuts? For years I had collected Chinese paper-cuts, fragile little works of art that resemble lace doilies, but mine were all of one color — red, black, or white — and all of quite traditional design, certainly nothing like these charming contemporary works done in such a brilliant range of colors. I was delighted.

Sometime later, a friend gave me a copy of Lafcadio Hearn's classic Japanese mystery *Earless Ho-ichi*, illustrated by Masakazu Kuwata — in *kiri-e*. The pictures marched; they curved; they swirled across the pages with an exquisite freedom I had never seen in the traditional paper-cuts of my own collection. I was fascinated.

I was so fascinated, I decided I absolutely had to learn more about this art form that so excited my imagination. I began seriously to search out information on *kiri-e* and was eventually able to obtain, from Tokyo, two volumes of *kiri-e* by Masayuki Miyata — and what a visual feast! The designs covered a fantastic range of emotions; they were happy, sad, spiritual, decadent, somber, brilliant. And I was hooked!

This was something I had to try for myself, so I began

another search, this time for materials explaining the techniques of paper-cutting. Unfortunately I found such material to be very scarce, and what I did find was limited almost exclusively to the techniques of traditional Chinese paper-cuts; instructions, usually consisting of no more than a paragraph or two, indicated that all you needed was a sharp knife, a pair of scissors, and some paper, and you were in business. The *kiri-e* I had seen—and the kind of thing I wanted to do—was certainly a bit more complicated than that. So I was left with a decision: Either forget the whole thing or work out the technique for myself. I decided to work it out.

I analyzed hundreds of pictures, discovering in the course of my study that the Chinese paper-cut was not limited to the one-color design with which I was familiar but that it, too, made use of different hues in various and delightful ways. I experimented and practiced until I was finally able to achieve the results I wanted.

I learned at a very early stage in my experimentation that I would have to make a few substitutions for some of the materials the Chinese and Japanese artists used. For example, many kinds of paper that exist in the Orient in a wide range of textures and colors are not readily available here in the West; but we do have very satisfactory stand-ins. One source indicated that the most important tool for paper-cutting was a working surface consisting of a shallow tray filled with melted animal fat thickened with finely powdered charcoal. Flouting this tradition, I have found that a magazine or a pad of newspaper serves the purpose quite well. I do not feel that such substitution destroys the "purity" of the art form. If it did, artists would still be grinding their pigments in the manner of Michelangelo and Leonardo.

Finally, believing that there are others who will derive the same pleasure I have found from this fascinating art form, I have set down the results of my several years of experimentation and practice, beginning with the simple, basic techniques that require only a "sharp knife, a pair of scissors, and some paper," and moving to more advanced techniques that involve applying color.

I sincerely hope that you will find as much enjoyment in this centuries-old—yet very contemporary—art form as I have. Happy cutting.

How to Use This Book

Cut-art can be divided into three basic types according to the techniques and materials used: monochrome, appliqué, and painted—in that order of difficulty. In the first part, we shall consider the fundamental techniques of monochrome cut-art; the second part introduces advanced techniques that involve color: appliqué, in which colored papers are applied to a design; and painted cut-art, in which paint is applied to a picture by various means. These advanced techniques allow greater freedom of design, particularly in Japanese *kiri-e*, where they can be used in combination to get especially intense color effects.

As you look briefly through this book, you will see that it consists of a series of projects that constitute separate chapters, each introducing a different technique or aspect of cut-art that is a bit more advanced than the previous one. Every chapter also contains designs with which to practice the technique just explained. Because the book is structured so that one lesson builds upon another, to get the most out of it I recommend that you follow this procedure:

- ☐ Follow the step-by-step instructions for completing the initial design in each chapter.
- ☐ After you have completed that design, carefully trace each of the practice designs and carry them out according to the instructions you used for the initial design.
- ☐ Using your imagination (or your files), create and complete a design similar to those you have just finished.
- ☐ Move on to the next chapter and follow the same procedure. No matter how advanced the technique, it will begin the same simple way—with a monochrome cut.

To begin, you will need to collect the basic supplies listed on pages 21–23. As you progress to the more advanced techniques of appliqué and painted cut-art, you will need additional supplies, which will vary from project to project and will be introduced as necessary. Be sure to check the materials list that precedes each project to make certain you have everything you need at hand.

Starting with the simple steps of Chapter 1, you will become involved with an art form that will give you hours of increasing enjoyment.

CHAPTER 1

A Short History of Cut-Art

According to a rather reliable legend, paper was invented in China about A.D. 105 by Ts'ai Lun, a court attendant to the Han emperor Ho Ti, who had become increasingly irritated at the difficulty of writing on bamboo strips or pieces of silk. Made of the inner bark of the mulberry tree, Ts'ai Lun's paper proved to be versatile and adaptable, but was very scarce and expensive. Because paper was available to only the wealthiest people, it is quite possible that the art of the paper-cut — in which a design or a picture is cut from a single sheet of paper in such a manner that it remains a continuous, connected whole — first developed as an aristocratic pastime.

Rosette and pairs of horses, sixth-century chung-hua *designs.*

Chinese Paper-Cuts

As the art of papermaking spread rapidly throughout China, paper soon became available to even the poorest individual, and the paper-cut developed into a traditional folk-art form. Originally called *chung-hua*, or "window flowers," these delicate and often intricate designs were carefully cut by hand with small, sharp knives or scissors to create decorations for windows — which were also made of paper.

Typical Chinese paper-cut.

The art of paper-cutting has been practiced in China for more than a thousand years. In 1959 archeologists working on site at Kaochang in western China's Xinjiang Uygur Region uncovered paper-cuts dating from A.D. 514 to 551. The various designs of rosettes, horses, and monkeys were skillfully done, indicating that the art of paper-cutting had been practiced for some time prior to the sixth century.

Kuan Yin, the Goddess of Mercy, and her disciple. This type of traditional paper-cut, called hua-yang, *was cut freehand with scissors and was used as an embroidery pattern for such small, everyday items as women's and children's footwear, caps, dresses, and aprons.*

Chinese shadow puppet.

It is presumed by some archeologists that these earliest paper-cuts were symbols used in religious functions. Later written records indicate that at least by the T'ang dynasty (608–906) the paper-cut had become a popular art form that was widespread enough for distinctive styles to have emerged, the designs of northern China featuring broad, forceful lines and those of southern China using fine, delicate lines. Subject matter was diverse and included such themes as real and mythical animals and birds; flowers and fruits of the countryside; children performing various activities; and historical, theatrical, and literary scenes. Some designs became so popular that they were given elaborate names like "Dragon and Phoenix," "Ploughing Ox and Harnessed Horse," and "Floating Clouds and Moving Moon." They were copied repeatedly, often to be handed down through several generations.

Paper windows were replaced at least once annually, usually at New Year's, and paper-cuts were most often used to adorn them but were also pasted to walls, ceilings, and other parts of the house. Smaller objects such as furniture, mirrors, lanterns and lamps, gift boxes, and food were decorated with the bright "window flowers" as well, and flowers of gold and silver paper became fashionable as accessories for the hair of both ladies and gentlemen of the court. In time, paper-cuts became an important part of Chinese birthdays, weddings, and funerals. Hundreds of itinerant craftsmen and small family "factories" supplied the ever-growing demand for the fragile decorations.

Paper-cut techniques and designs — the sawtooth patterns, the crescents, the whorls and flowers — eventually found their way into other Chinese arts and crafts, including metalwork and leather and lacquer work. In embroidery paper-cuts were pasted onto pieces of silk and sewn over with thread; in pottery and textile work, they were used as stencils for glazes and dyes. Paper-cutting techniques were even used in the theater to create the leather-cut puppets for a popular form of drama that still exists today.

Eventually, as China opened her doors to trade with other countries, paper manufacture and the art of the paper-cut moved beyond Chinese boundaries and began to affect the arts of other countries as well.

Japanese Paper-Cuts

By the beginning of the Heian period (794–1185), Japan's great, golden era of artistic development, paper had become an important aspect of aristocratic culture, as a reading of such early literary works as Lady Murasaki's *Tale of Genji* and Sei Shonagon's *Pillow Book* will clearly show. Japanese craftsmen soon outstripped their Chinese counterparts by creating paper of such high quality and wide variety that it is still considered to be the world's finest. The Japanese, however, did more than just that; they also established a cultural practice that added a further dimension to the art of the paper-cut.

Toward the middle of the Heian period, high-ranking members of the imperial court—"People Who Dwell Above the Clouds," as they were called—began wearing special textile designs on their court robes to indicate family or clan relationship. Displaying such symbols was encouraged by the powerful Fujiwara clan then ruling the country. Called *mon*, this family crest was placed on all robes worn for formal and state occasions—one on the back, centered between the shoulder blades; one on the back of each sleeve; and, for the most important occasions, one over each breast—a total of five *mon*.

Mon of Japan's greatest military leaders.

Hollyhock, Tokugawa Ieyasu (1542–1616).

Paulownia plant, Toyotomi Hideyoshi (1536–1598).

Papaya cross-section, Oda Nobunaga (1534–1582).

Variations on a mon *based on Japanese clover.*

The main household or most powerful family of a clan had its own crest; lesser members wore variations of this design. Each aristocratic family had two different *mon*—a *jōmon* for important occasions, and a *kayemon* for everyday use.

As elegant as the people who wore them, *mon* were usually refined, abstract designs based on such natural objects as lotus blossoms, plum and cherry blossoms, and bellflowers. In the beginning, these designs were not embroidered on the robes but were dyed on using a stencil. It was the creation of the *mon* and the cutting of the stencil for it that were responsible, as far as history tells us, for the first truly Japanese development in the art of the paper-cut—*mon-kiri*, or "crest-cut."

After the fall of the Heian court and the rise of the military government of the Kamakura period (1185–1333), the use of the *mon* became more widespread. The daimyos, ruling lords of the various feudal provinces, adopted the *mon* as a form of family identification, placing the symbol on banners, flags, and weapons to distinguish their camps and troops during battle. The warriors, or samurai, were allowed to use a variation of the *mon* of the daimyo to whom they had given allegiance.

The following period, the Muromachi (1336–1573), was an era of frequent wars, and massed battles replaced single combat as the common form of warfare. The *mon* thus became even more important as a means for identifying opposing forces on the battlefield, and was simplified so as to be

Katazome *(stencil-dyed) material used as a chest cover.*

conspicuous and instantly recognizable.

During the Edo, or Tokugawa, period (1600–1867) Japan moved into an era of peace, and the individual family crest returned to prominence, not only among aristocrats but among the merchant class and other commoners as well. The designs were now embroidered on rather than dyed into the fabric of a kimono. Simple symmetrical motifs prevailed, and surrounding these with a circle became very popular.

Chrysanthemum mon *of Japan's imperial family.*

Crane (tsuru) *trademark of Japan Air Lines. Reproduced by permission.*

Trademark of Takashimaya Co., Ltd., a Tokyo-based department-store chain. Reproduced by permission.

It was also during this period that the paper-cut achieved a high point in practical as well as artistic development, thanks to its application to the art of stencil-dyed textiles (*katazome*). Stencils had been employed in textile design in a rather simple manner prior to this time, but during the seventeenth century they began to be used widely to create highly detailed and exquisite patterns so technically complicated that in 1892 one Westerner wrote: "That anyone but a Japanese could execute such difficult work as this is simply impossible."

Made from paper used previously for other purposes, stencils allowed textile manufacturers to add all kinds of designs to their fabrics, from elegantly simple borders to lavish overall patterns, in one or several colors. They were also used to make *kakemono*—hanging picture scrolls on which the basic designs were stenciled first and the final details added with brush and ink.

In the country's Meiji period (1868–1912) various business organizations, industries, and corporations grew in prominence, and many of them designed *mon*, counterparts to Western trademarks. Simple, familiar images such as geese, snowflakes, drums, and rabbits served as the basis for many of the designs; no form of the chrysanthemum was permitted, however, as this was the crest of the imperial family.

It was also during this period that the art of the paper-cut moved beyond *mon-kiri* to *kiri-gami*, or "cut paper," in which the paper is folded and the design cut with scissors in a manner similar to the method children use today to make paper dolls and snowflakes. The art of *kiri-gami* is still taught in the early grades of Japanese schools to encourage not only artistic development but also an awareness of the national heritage.

Western Paper-Cuts

At the same time that the art of the paper-cut was achieving its greatest popularity in Japan, it was achieving a similar popularity in Europe. No one knows exactly how the art of paper-

Pattern used in katazome *(stencil dyeing).*

making reached the West from China; however, historical records indicate that there were paper mills in Spain and Italy in 1150; in France in 1189; in Germany in 1291; and in England in 1330. The first paper mill in the United States was built in 1690.

Created during the Middle Ages, the first Western papercuts were, according to historical accounts, "prayer pictures" — religious scenes cut and painted and offered as gifts in commemoration of sacred events. By the end of the medieval period, the practice had become a secular art form, developing into what the Poles called *wycinanki* and the Germans called *Scherenschnitte*; designs were based on scenes from nature and from fairy tales and folklore.

This technique was brought to the United States in about 1683, when German and Swiss refugees fleeing religious persecution in Europe settled in Pennsylvania on the invitation of William Penn. These were the people who eventually became known as the "Pennsylvania Dutch" (a corruption of *deutsch*, meaning German).

In addition to displaying skill in the art of *Scherenschnitte*, many of these people — particularly schoolteachers and craftsmen — were proficient in Fractur, a decorative and elegant style of calligraphy. These two art forms were often combined in the decoration of baptismal certificates, or *Taufscheine*, as well as birth and wedding certificates. Later the art adorned furniture and pottery, and on buildings it appeared in the form of large hex signs consisting of elaborate and brightly painted

Pennsylvania Dutch hex sign.

geometric motifs intended to ward off evil spirits.

The next development in the art of the paper-cut occurred in Europe, where, from the middle of the eighteenth century until about 1860, silhouettes were a popular craze. Named after Etienne de Silhouette, France's controller general of finances under Louis XV, the earliest such paper-cuts were life-size; these were eventually replaced by smaller, more delicate works of art that took on aspects of portraiture and were often referred to as "profiles in miniature."

Scherenschnitte *design.*

Contemporary silhouette.

Although making silhouettes retained some popularity through the 1920s — particularly in Germany, where special machines were built to produce them — the paper-cut was effectively killed as a folk-art form — as were many other folk arts — upon the advent in Europe of the Industrial Revolution in the mid–nineteenth century.

Mexican paper-cut.

Contemporary Paper-Cuts

Although the art of paper-cutting is still practiced in such diverse areas of the world as England, Malaysia, and Mexico, we must turn our attention once more to China and Japan to see how the art has been revitalized in recent times.

During the Ch'ing dynasty (1644–1912), when China was ruled by a foreign power, the native arts, including the paper-cut, declined. In 1940, however, members of the Lu Hsun Art Academy and the Peking Institute of Fine Art rediscovered the old art form and brought new themes to it.

The People's Republic of China, born in 1949, placed great emphasis on "art for the masses." The government employed the most gifted of the surviving folk artists as teachers, and studies of the age-old art of paper-cutting were documented in numerous books. During the early years after the revolution the paper-cut was but one medium for propaganda, and images of bridge and factory construction and children practicing guerilla warfare were the norm. With the overthrow of the Gang of Four in the 1970s, however, the art form was freed to go in other directions, and today in China paper-cuts illustrate books, magazines, and newspapers and are used as designs on stationery and even postage stamps.

It is in Japan that the greatest revitalization has occurred. New ideas and techniques from such creative artists as Kuwata and Miyata have lifted the paper-cut from the level of folk art to that of an exciting fine art now known as *kiri-e*, or "cut-art."

Propagandistic Chinese paper-cut.

Postage stamp from the People's Republic of China based on a paper-cut design.

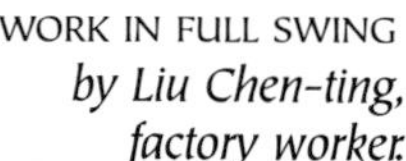

WORK IN FULL SWING
by Liu Chen-ting, factory worker.

CHAPTER 2

BITTER HARVEST.

Getting Started

I DON'T RECALL where I first heard it, but there is an old Chinese story that clearly dramatizes the basic requirement for getting started in — and staying with — cut-art. According to this story, a man traveling in a rural area of China one day came upon an elderly peasant woman sitting at the side of the path, slowly and patiently rubbing a large iron crowbar on a sandstone rock. Puzzled by her actions, the traveler approached and asked the woman what she was doing, to which she replied that she had lost her only embroidery needle and was rubbing the crowbar on the rock to make a new one.

Chinese opera mask.

The point of the story is, of course, patience, and above all else, cut-art requires just that: the patience to sit quietly for whatever time is required and, with steady hands, to complete the project you have set out to do. This doesn't mean that you are going to work for hours at a time to finish an image in one sitting. In fact, unless the design is a fairly simple one, I strongly recommend that you *don't* try to complete it in one sitting. Nothing is going to deter you more from the practice of cut-art than sitting for hours and laboring until your fingers, your back, and your neck become stiff and sore.

If you become tired, stop; put the work away and plan to resume it at another time. One of the beauties of cut-art is that, like knitting, crocheting, and needlepoint, it can be worked on or set aside at your leisure. Unlike painting or sculpture or pottery, cut-art means there is no paint to thicken, no clay to harden; the work will be exactly as you left it.

When I say that you must have patience, I mean simply that there are no shortcuts. From sad experience, I have found that any attempt at haste, any attempt to speed the process usually results in the loss of several hours' worth of effort. If you have an intricate and involved design, it is better to spread the work out over many hours — or even days — than to try to rush through and risk ruining it.

For all the time and patience required, however, particularly with the advanced techniques, cut-art can be very relaxing mentally. There is pleasure in the involvement, a great sense of personal satisfaction in seeing a work of art evolve before your eyes that seems to release the tensions of daily living; and it can also lead to an esthetic fulfillment that is often lacking in our lives.

Cut-art *is* an art form, but you certainly do not have to be an artist either to enjoy it or to create it. I have had students in the classroom who would insist that they had never been able to do anything artistic in their lives, yet who, when introduced to cut-art, would create beautiful and imaginative pictures and designs. Ideas for cut-art appear in abundance — a particular iris that suddenly catches your attention, the pattern made by the shadow of the garden gate, a figurine or statue you have overlooked before, an illustration or photograph in a magazine; and the more you become involved in cut-art, the more you will grow in awareness of the designs and patterns of the environment that surrounds you.

Soon after you become aware of a particular image, you should record it in a quick, rough sketch and file it away for future reference. And I should emphasize *rough* sketch, because you are not attempting a completed work of art here; you are merely setting down the outlines of an idea so that you will have something to jog your memory later when you are ready to begin your design.

TORI TO HANA.

I also suggest that you keep a file of clippings — newspaper photographs, magazine illustrations — that inspire ideas or designs you might incorporate into pictures at a later date. Your final work may be made up of elements drawn from one or perhaps several images you have collected. Most successful artists work from models rather than trust their memories to remind them how a hand looks in a certain position, or the way a head looks when held at a particular angle. The clippings and sketches you gather will serve as your models for future work.

At least in the beginning, I encourage you to copy. Copy designs; copy parts of pictures; copy complete pictures, making certain that you pay close attention to the way the artist or photographer has arranged the details in his work. Every artist copies at one time or another, so why should you be different? Copying is also part of the Chinese art tradition, at least as far back as the sixth century; in the last of his "Six Canons of Art," the master artist Hsieh Ho stated that copying was the only method for learning the basic techniques of art.

The interesting thing about copying is that you will soon become aware of the completely different appearance your paper-cut has from the original photograph or picture; this is due to differences in the materials and techniques involved, and to the adjustments that must be made in transferring an image from one medium to another. Of course, as your confidence and your abilities grow, you will become less and less dependent on other sources and will refer to your files merely to find the model for a hand or a particular flower as you sketch your own original designs.

And sketch you must! Even the most adept and professional paper-cut artists use sketches; some of these, as we saw in the previous chapter, have been handed down over several generations. Because of the intricacy and detail of most cut-art, it is exceedingly difficult to work freehand. It is also a good idea to make two copies of a sketch before you begin to incorporate it in your paper-cut — one for immediate use, and one to be filed away should you wish to make further copies of your design or damage your first attempt.

Now that these psychological aspects of cut-art have been considered, we must next turn our attention to its physical aspects — that is, to the materials it involves.

Basic Materials for Cut-Art

The actual materials for cut-art are both inexpensive and, in most cases, easily obtainable. Some you may already have in your home; others may be found in almost any art, craft, or department store. In addition, at the back of this book I have listed several suppliers who will be happy to assist you by mail.

Knives. Most cut-art is done with a sharp knife, so this is one of the first items you will want to obtain. One of the most satisfactory cutting tools is a #1 X-Acto knife with a #11 blade. (You will also want to purchase a supply of extra blades.) If you have access to a surgical supply company, a scalpel with replaceable blades is another excellent and inexpensive cutting tool. You may also wish to purchase a set of small wood-cutting tools, which are particularly useful for creating curves, V-shapes, and the like.

Scissors. You will need two pairs of scissors, one large and one small. For the large pair, 6–8″ (15.2–20.3 cm) paper or desk shears work the best. Check to make certain that the handles fit comfortably over your fingers and that they make a clean cut from the rivet to the tip. Some inexpensive scissors cut only part way, and this could result in a torn edge rather than in a smooth, clean cut. For the small scissors, you will need a pair about 3½″ (8.9 cm) in length. Because

Typical Chinese paper-cut.

these are used for small details, I prefer curved cuticle scissors, which work well for cutting rounded shapes like curves and scallops. This, however, is merely a matter of personal preference. Whatever kind you get, again, make certain that the handles fit your fingers comfortably and that the cut the scissors make is sharp and clean.

Scissors used in cut-art should not be used for any purpose other than cutting paper, since the blades easily become dull. Always keep your scissors sharp and well oiled, but take care to wipe them completely clean, since any excess oil will stain a paper-cut.

Paper. Paper is certainly no problem; it is available everywhere, from the brown sack you brought home from the grocery store to the wrapping on your last birthday gift. However, for the projects you intend to keep, you will certainly want to obtain some of the many special papers that will give your work a more professional appearance.

CONSTRUCTION PAPER. The most readily available of all the special papers, construction paper comes in a broad range of colors, usually several to a package, although packages of one color are also available. Because of its rather loose weave, however, construction paper does not lend itself well to designs that require fine, delicate lines. It works best where broad lines prevail or where color is to be appliquéd. A sharp blade is an absolute necessity when using construction paper, since a dull blade will easily fray or tear the edges of the cut.

ORIGAMI PAPER. Traditionally used in Japanese paper-folding, origami paper lends itself beautifully to cut-art. Usually sold in packages of 100 to 125 sheets, it comes in a wide range of colors; the reverse side of each colored sheet is white. This thin, strong paper works well in designs that require a delicacy and intricacy of line, and in projects where multiple copies are made in one cutting. Origami paper is available in most art supply stores and Oriental specialty shops.

SCHERENSCHNITTE PAPER. This paper is made especially for cut-

Chinese paper-cut of Nanking Bridge.

art work and usually comes in packets of six colors: black, red, blue, gray, green, and brown. It is widely available in most art and craft shops.

GIFT WRAP. Plain, unpatterned gift wrap is another excellent and inexpensive material. Although it may be a bit more limited in color range than some other kinds of paper, it should certainly be used whenever possible. As we shall see later, metallic-foil wrap lends a note of special elegance to some cut-art.

SPECIALTY PAPERS. In addition to the papers already mentioned, you will certainly wish to try some of the specialty papers—particularly the wide range of handmade Japanese papers available through a number of art supply companies. Many papers designed for other types of artwork also lend themselves well to cut-art. One of my favorites is Canson Mi-Teintes, a paper widely used for charcoal and pastel drawing, printmaking, and book arts. It is available through art supply stores in several sizes and colors.

WHITE TYPEWRITER PAPER. You will need lots of this—white bond, not erasable or onionskin typewriter paper—for making sketches and patterns. Buy the most inexpensive brand you can find.

TRACING PAPER. This is a necessity for copying a design or picture from a book or other source that you do not wish to damage. Simply place the tracing paper over the picture and lightly trace the outlines.

CARBON PAPER. You will need this in conjunction with white typewriter paper when tracing a design on whose surface you can draw directly with a pen or pencil. The carbon and paper are simply slipped underneath the design you are copying. Carbon paper is also essential for creating symmetrical designs. Pencil carbon paper is preferable, as it makes a line with less pressure than typewriter carbon.

NEWSPAPERS, MAGAZINES, AND GIFT CATALOGS. Stacks of these make excellent cutting pads. And what better way to make use of the daily newspaper and all those magazines and gift catalogs that stuff the mailbox every day? Those made of soft, pulpy paper are better as cutting pads than those with a slick, hard finish, which can dull your cutting blade fairly quickly.

Mounting Board. You will certainly want to mount some of your cuts for permanent display, and will need something stiff and durable like bristol board or pasteboard. I find, however, that for most such purposes plain white or pastel-colored 10-ply poster board works best. It is rather inexpensive and more readily available than other types of mounting board.

Acetate Folders. Made of clear plastic, acetate folders — the kind used to cover loose-leaf pages — are excellent for protecting finished cuts or for temporarily displaying pictures. They are usually available wherever stationery supplies are sold.

Adhesives. Adhesives are essential for gluing paper-cuts to mounting boards, as well as for appliqué techniques. Here are several possibilities.

RUBBER CEMENT. This adhesive is made especially for use with paper and comes in small bottles with a brush applicator or in large cans. Since rubber cement does have a tendency to thicken, I do not recommend the can size unless you also invest in a can of thinner. One advantage of rubber cement is that it can be removed quite easily from most surfaces with an eraser. One disadvantage, however, is that over time it will turn brown and may even stain your paper-cut.

WATER-SOLUBLE WHITE GLUE. The best-known brand is Elmer's Glue-All. While it may be used as is for heavier work, I recommend that for delicate work you pour a small amount into a saucer or other open container and add a few drops of boiling water to thin it. Apply this type of glue with a fine-tip watercolor brush. Its one disadvantage is that if you are using colored paper for your cut, you must be careful not to get too much glue on it, as this can cause the color to bleed onto your mounting board or other parts of the design.

GLUE STICKS. Available in several different brands and sizes, the glue stick is a versatile and simple means for mounting paper-cuts. I prefer the small tube, since it is easier to work with when handling delicate cuts.

SPRAYS. Spray adhesives offer a quick and efficient way to mount full-color paper-cuts to board but require a bit more practice in handling when you are mounting monochrome paper-cuts, which have a smaller surface area. Try sprays first on cuts that have broad lines and minimal detail.

Other Materials. In addition to the materials already listed, there are several miscellaneous items you will want to consider:

PENCILS for tracing and sketching. While any pencil will do, a #2 pencil gives the darkest line with the least amount of pressure. This is especially important when you are drawing a pattern on the back of a cutout; too much pressure will cause the paper to tear.

SEVERAL FINE-TIP BRUSHES for applying adhesives. Applicator brushes in containers of rubber cement are usually too wide for fine detail work.

ERASERS for removing excess rubber cement. I personally prefer a pencil-shaped typewriter eraser, since the fine tip gets into all the little curves and grooves of a design with ease.

MASKING OR TRANSPARENT TAPE for attaching a pattern to your cutting pad and attaching a traced design to your paper.

A SMOOTH PIECE OF WOOD for a cutting board; this is placed under your pad of newspaper. Another excellent cutting board can be fashioned from a plastic turntable like those sold by Rubbermaid. Or, you may wish to purchase an inexpensive self-sealing cutting base from an art supply store. These mats allow cut marks to heal completely, and last for years. You will not need a newspaper or magazine pad if you use a cutting base such as this.

A PAPER PUNCH for making small circles. The combination punch for paper and leather, with six holes of different sizes, permits the greatest versatility.

PART ONE

BASIC TECHNIQUES: MONOCHROME CUT-ART

CHAPTER 3

Silhouettes

FIRST POPULARIZED in Europe, the silhouette is also a part of the Japanese art tradition; and, because it is among the easiest forms of cut-art to create, we shall begin with it.

A silhouette is basically the "shadow" of an object cut from paper of a solid color—usually black—and mounted on a white background. Most portrait silhouettes are done in profile; rarely is the full-front view used. This limits to some extent the kinds of things that can be depicted in silhouette, but this art form nonetheless does offer interesting possibilities for rather delightful pictures. And for our purposes, it affords excellent practice in the use of scissors for cut-art.

MATERIALS

- Tracing paper
- Soft-lead pencil
- Origami paper (optional)
- Carbon paper (optional; pencil carbon is preferable)
- Black paper
- Masking or transparent tape
- Two pairs of scissors, one large, one small
- Cutting knife

PRACTICE DESIGN

CUTTING WITH SCISSORS

As you cut, hold the scissors still and feed the paper into them with your hand, turning the paper, not the scissors as you progress through a design. Cut with the full blade of the scissors, not the point; the point is used only when you are finishing a tight spot in a cut.

Some silhouettes involve cuts inside the design (for example, the space between the front legs of the prancing horse on page 29). A cut such as this should be made first; start it with your cutting knife, then finish it with the scissors. Never start an inside cut by poking through the paper with the scissor point.

1. Place the sheet of tracing paper over the practice design shown above.
2. With a soft-lead pencil, carefully trace the outline of the silhouette onto the tracing paper. *Note:* If you are using origami paper, which is white on the back, you can transfer the outline carefully onto the white side with carbon paper. Remember that in doing so, the finished picture will be the reverse of the traced outline.
3. So that you will not waste a full sheet of your black paper, cut a square from it that is just slightly larger than the outline.
4. Cut the tracing paper, with the outline fairly well centered, to the same size as your black paper.
5. Tape the two sheets of paper together with small pieces of masking or transparent tape. (This will not be necessary if you transferred the outline onto origami paper.) To keep the two sheets securely attached as you cut out the silhouette, place a piece of tape on each corner and in the middle of each of the four sides.
6. Because the details of the practice design are rather large, cut out the silhouette with your large scissors, beginning at the point of the collar.
7. Now that you have completed the practice design, follow the same steps for the additional silhouettes included in this chapter. Because the details in these are smaller, they should be cut out with the smaller scissors, using the same procedure as that described in the box.
8. Once you have completed the silhouettes, file them away neatly until you are ready to mount them. They are best kept in acetate folders or envelopes; however, they can also be filed away between sheets of clean typewriter paper and placed in a manila folder. Always store them flat so that they do not curl or wrinkle.

Creating Your Own Silhouettes

Creating your own silhouettes is not difficult. Anything that makes an interesting shadow can be used as a pattern; small, unique objects found around the home make much more interesting and artistic silhouettes than very large items. The silhouettes I have included here were created from several Japanese and Chinese figurines I have in my studio.

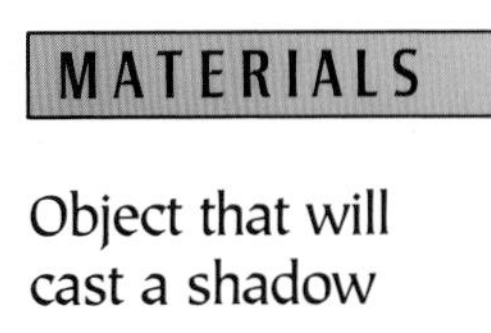

MATERIALS

Object that will cast a shadow

Masking tape

White paper

Light source

Soft-lead pencil

PROCEDURE

1. Choose the object you wish to use as the basis for your silhouette.
2. With masking tape, fasten a sheet of white paper to the wall.
3. Place the object to be shadowed a few inches in front of the sheet of white paper.
4. Place the light source directly opposite the object and adjust both until the object throws a sharp, distinct shadow onto the paper. You will need to experiment a bit. Too bright a light source will diffuse the shadow. A 25-watt bulb in an unshaded reading lamp placed approximately 4′ (1.22 m) from the object is usually adequate. Make certain that the light source is directly in front of the object. If it is above or below it, the shadow will be distorted. Work in a room that is at least semidark, where distracting side lighting that might diffuse the shadow is cut off.
5. Stand or sit to one side of the object, making certain that your arm or hand does not intrude upon the shadow; then carefully trace the outline of the shadow onto the white paper. In your first attempt, you may find that your lines tend to waver. If so, once you finish the outline, remove the paper from the wall and, leaving the object in place so that you can check the details, straighten out any places where you strayed from the shadow. With practice you should soon be able to draw strong, unwavering lines.
6. Follow steps 4–8 of the first procedure for cutting out a silhouette.

PRACTICE DESIGNS

CHAPTER 4

Geometric and Abstract Designs

GEOMETRIC DESIGNS are based on the repetition of straight lines, triangles, circles, or similar regular forms, or on a combination of these forms. In cut-art geometric elements are usually incorporated within a larger design and form the repeating patterns of such motifs as fences and tiled roofs. Although used less often as the basis for a total design, geometric shapes can be very effective by themselves and can result in images that are highly reminiscent of the abstract woodblock prints of such contemporary Japanese artists as Masaji Yoshida, Masao Ohba, and Kunihiro Amano.

For our purposes the geometric design will serve as an introduction to the use of the cutting knife.

MATERIALS

- Tracing paper
- Soft-lead pencil
- Colored paper
- Masking or transparent tape
- Cutting pad and board, or self-sealing base
- Cutting knife (X-Acto knife or surgical scalpel)

PRACTICE DESIGN

1. Using the practice design above, follow steps 1–5 in the procedure for cutting out silhouettes in Chapter 3: Trace the design and center the pattern over a sheet of colored paper.
2. Tape your pattern and the colored paper together at each corner with masking or transparent tape.
3. Tape the pattern and the colored paper securely to a cutting pad made of newspaper or a magazine, or to a self-sealing cutting base.
4. If you are using a newspaper or magazine pad, place it on a wooden cutting board or a plastic turntable.
5. Using your knife, cut out the design. Do the smallest sections first, beginning in the middle and working outward.
6. Follow the same steps for the additional designs.

CUTTING WITH A KNIFE

Hold your knife as you would a pen or pencil. Try to keep an even, constant pressure on the knife from the beginning to the end of the cut, and use only the point.

When making a straight cut, try to avoid removing or lifting the knife from the paper before the cut is finished. When cutting circles or curves, you will get a sharper edge if you turn the paper as you cut. A rotating surface such as a plastic turntable is especially helpful for this.

When making inside cuts, be certain that the cut ends *exactly* at the point where it began; otherwise you might tear or fray the paper or leave an unsightly tick when you try to remove the cutout portion.

As you work, press down on the paper with your fingers as close as possible to the line you are cutting. This will reduce tension on the paper and make it less liable to tear. Do be careful, though; knives and scalpels are very sharp, and we want no sliced fingers!

As soon as you begin having difficulty cutting a line, change your blade. A dull blade can easily fray or tear a design.

Creating Your Own Geometric and Abstract Designs

Geometric designs are even easier to create than silhouettes. All you have to do is look around; there are patterns everywhere if you will only become aware of them. The pattern for the practice design on page 32, for example, was suggested by moonlight shining through the winter-bare branches of the birch tree in my garden; the additional designs were suggested by other, equally obvious sights: a ladybug, sunrise over a mountain, and ripples in a pool.

MATERIALS

In addition to the materials already listed for this chapter, you will need:

Ruler

Draftsman's compass,
or round objects like lids or saucers to use as patterns for circles and curves

PROCEDURE

1. Observe your surroundings carefully for pattern ideas. They may come from completely unexpected sources—books on a shelf, a fence, perhaps the doodle on your telephone pad.
2. Once you discover a pattern, make a rough sketch of it immediately. Remember: All lines must connect so that your completed design will be in one piece.
3. After you make the rough sketch, straighten lines and smooth out curves and circles with the ruler and compass.
4. Follow the same procedure you used for the practice and additional designs.

PRACTICE DESIGNS

CHAPTER 5

Mon-Kiri

As we saw in the chapter on the history of cut-art, *mon-kiri* was an important aspect of this art form's development in Japan; today it is still very much a part of Japanese tradition. In 1913 the Matsuya Piece-Goods Store in Tokyo made a comprehensive compilation of *mon* in use at that time, a collection totaling 4,260 crests. Since then that number has grown considerably and is still growing as more and more businesses adopt *mon* as trademarks. The materials needed for this project are the same as those for Chapters 3 and 4.

PRACTICE DESIGN

PROCEDURE

Using your knife to make the inside cuts and your scissors to make the outside cuts, execute the practice design shown here following the same steps you did for the designs in the previous two chapters.

Creating Your Own Mon

Designing *mon* is not as difficult as it may first appear. Creating a personal symbol can be quite interesting; you can use the result for identification in the same manner the Japanese have traditionally used their crests. I liked the *mon* I designed for myself so well that I copyrighted it and use it on such things as my stationery, note cards, and book covers. The *mon* can also be enlarged and appliquéd or embroidered to make interesting pillow covers or wall hangings. Its use is limited only by your imagination.

Although some of the early *mon* were quite elaborate (for example, the umbrella on page 34), modern designs tend to be rather simple and straightforward. Many *mon* are variations on earlier designs; it is interesting to note, for instance, that in the 4,260 *mon* Matsuya compiled in 1913 there were only 204 basic motifs. So the design possibilities are quite limitless.

As with the geometric patterns of the last chapter, ideas for *mon* designs exist all around you. The practice and additional designs in this chapter, for example, are based on a horse's head, the initials JC, a basketball, and ocean waves against the moon. You might just as easily base designs on a dog's head, a tennis racket, a rose, or anything else that inspires you.

So, the first step in creating your own *mon* is to look at your environment and consider whatever in life interests you most. On a sheet of paper, list all the things you can think of that you really like—favorite flowers, sports, musical instruments—anything. Do you like to bowl or golf? List it. Do you like to play the guitar? List it. Did you have a passion for playing marbles or jacks when you were a kid? List it.

Once your list is finished, think through each item carefully. Which ones represent you most fully? Remember, in Japan the *mon* was meant to identify an individual or family, just as the heraldic symbol functioned in Europe. With what would you like to be identified? Try to reduce your list to three or four items.

Next, try to visualize each object as a simple, abstract design. What kind of shape will you give the *mon* as a whole? Although the circle is the most popular shape, triangles, squares, and even hexagons have been used. Imagine your design within these various shapes.

Draw a rough sketch of each design, remembering that all the lines must be connected so that the completed *mon* will be of one piece. Some ideas simply will not work out, and you will need to rework or discard several designs until you hit upon the one you feel is just right. Then proceed to complete the *mon* by following the steps you have already learned in the previous chapters.

From the desk of - - -
J.A.CHRISTENSEN

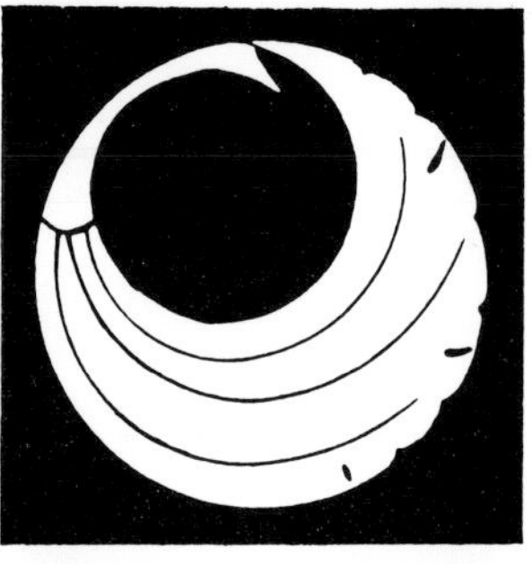

Variations on two motifs from ancient mon.

Making Multiple Copies

From time to time you may wish to make multiple copies of a design such as your *mon*. Chinese *hsuan* and *yu k'ou* papers make it possible to produce 100 copies in one cutting, but unfortunately these papers are unavailable to us. With origami paper, however, it is possible to make up to five copies in one cutting.

MATERIALS

In addition to materials already mentioned, you will need:

Large needle

Length of strong sewing thread

Drawing or dressmaker's pin

PROCEDURE

1. Prepare your pattern as you have already learned to do. Because of the amount of tension applied to the paper during cutting, patterns with wide lines hold up better than those with thin lines.
2. Cut your pattern and the cutting sheets to the same size.
3. With the needle and thread, firmly sew together all the sheets of paper, including your pattern. Sew around all four edges.
4. Using transparent or masking tape, attach the sewn sheets to the cutting pad to ensure that they will remain securely in place. Sheets should not be able to shift during cutting.
5. With a sharp blade, cut out each section of the design, applying enough pressure to go through all the sheets.
6. Use the pin to remove the cutout sections of the design.

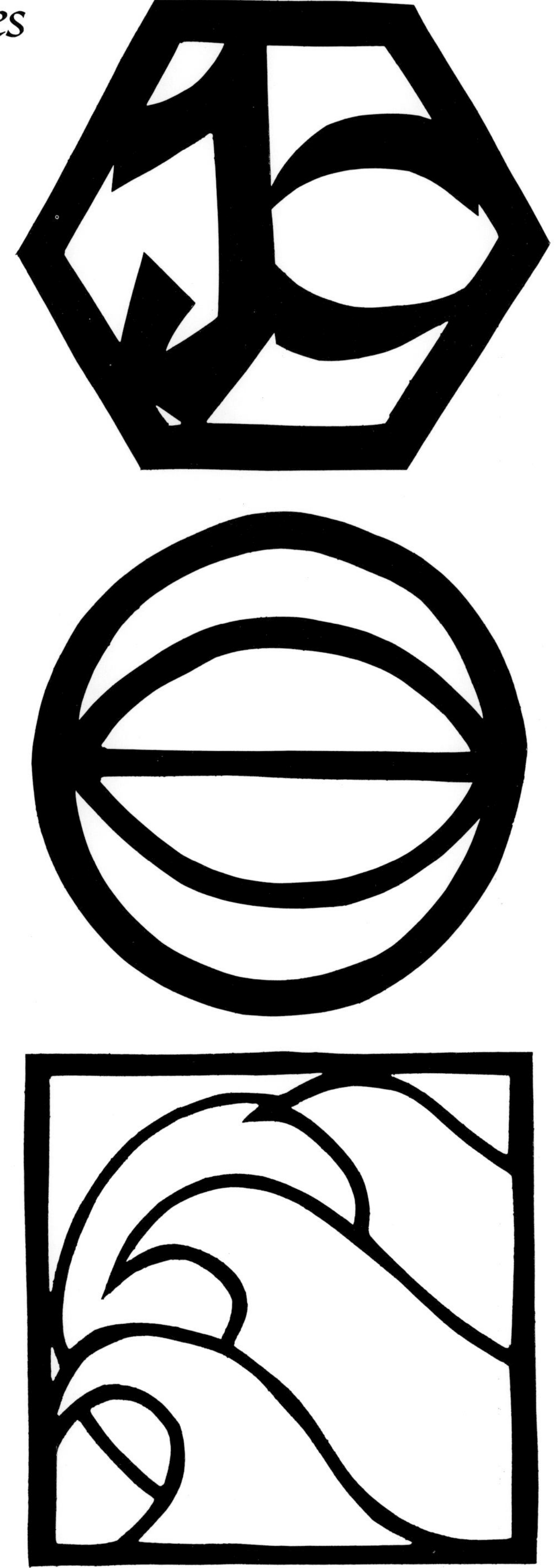

PRACTICE DESIGNS

CHAPTER 6

Copying

AS WE LEARNED earlier, copying, according to Chinese tradition and the teachings of the artist Hsieh Ho, is the only method for learning the basic techniques of art. Copying also makes it possible for anyone who is not necessarily a proficient artist to enjoy the pleasures of making paper-cuts. You can make an exact copy of another paper-cut fairly simply; reproducing an image from a painting, photograph, or other medium, however, cannot be done directly and usually requires some adjustments to the original design in order for the paper-cut to be executed in its traditional one-piece form. Becoming aware of these adjustments will be our major concern in this chapter.

MATERIALS

In addition to the basic materials you have already used in the previous chapters, you will need:

Picture to copy

Felt-tip pen

Paper-cut based on the Chinese ivory carving shown on page 40.

PROCEDURE

1. Choose a picture or design you would like to copy, such as the ivory carving example shown below, or use the practice design on page 43.
2. Using tracing paper or carbon and typewriter paper, make a clear outline of the picture, including all the necessary details, as shown at the top of the page opposite.
3. At this point, after you have drawn the design, you must consider what adjustments will be necessary to create a one-piece picture. If you study the original copy of the ivory statue on page 41 (top) carefully, you will see that there are a number of disconnected lines that float freely in the design. These must be joined with others to form a continuous whole. To do this, go over the design and draw in bars to connect any disjointed lines to continuous ones. In the example at the bottom of page 41, the connecting bars that were added appear in red. The design has now been adjusted so that it is all in one piece.
4. Once the adjustments have been made to the copy, go over all the lines with a felt-tip pen. This will help you double-check that all adjustments have been made; and, because the ink widens the line to more closely approximate the final cut, you will also be able to see if any necessary details might become lost in the cutting.
5. Following the steps you learned in the previous chapters, make the final cutout, as shown on page 38.
6. Following the steps outlined above, complete the practice design on page 43. You will note that this design is neither Chinese nor Japanese. I have chosen it on purpose to underscore the fact that although the techniques we are using are drawn from Oriental sources, the designs do not have to be.

CHANG NGO FLIES TO THE MOON, *ivory carving by anonymous artist, Beijing.*

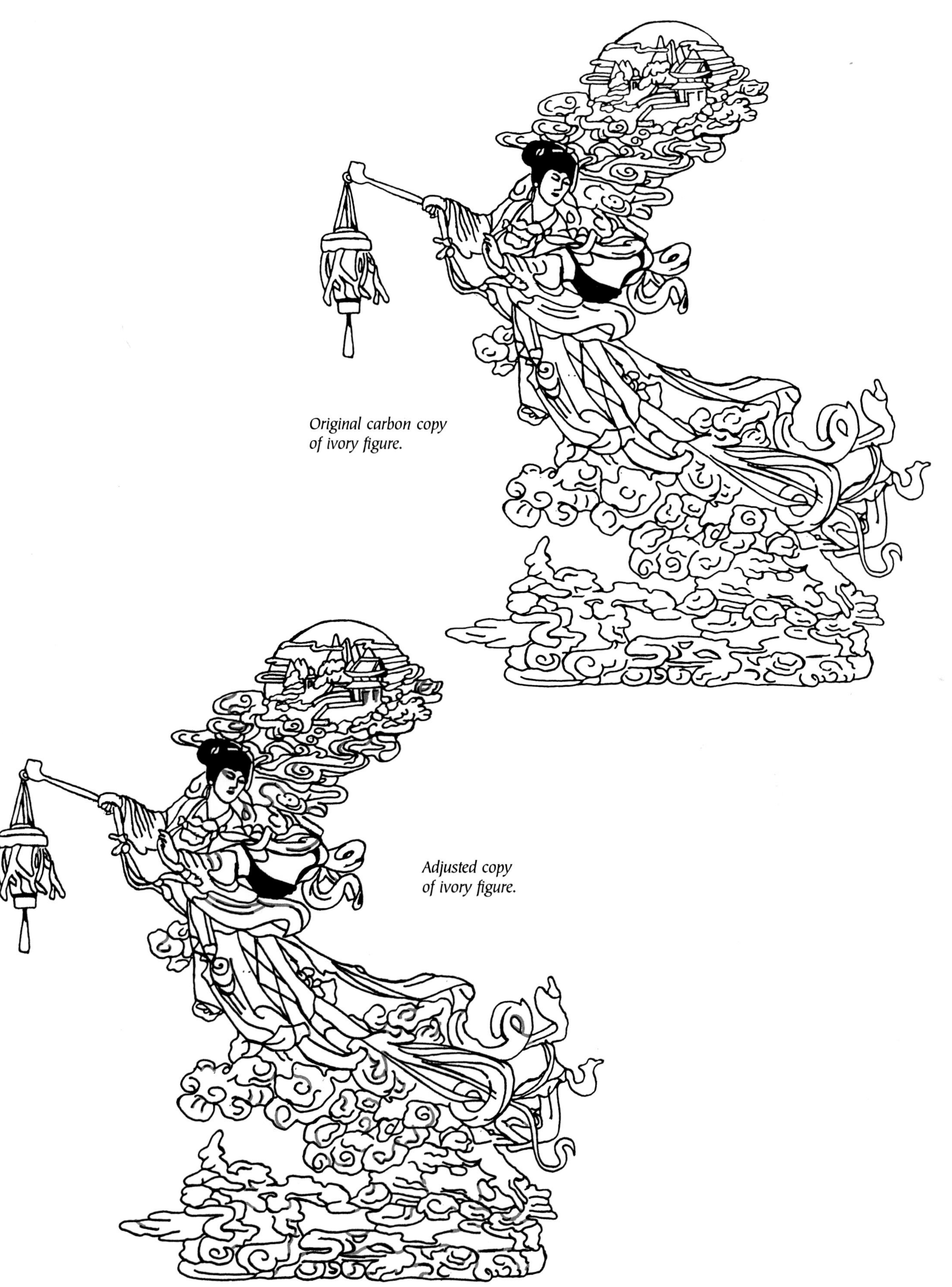

Original carbon copy of ivory figure.

Adjusted copy of ivory figure.

ADJUSTING FACIAL FEATURES

In the drawing of the ivory figure example, the eyes, nose, and mouth are simple, connected lines. In a larger picture, where these features are shown in greater detail, such treatment is not particularly effective. Paper-cut artists have thus developed different techniques that permit greater expression while solving the problem of adjusting facial features so that they connect to one another and are also tied to the rest of the picture, as the following examples show.

FRONT VIEW

Original wood-block print from which copy is to be made.

Here I have merely adjusted the hairline to form the connecting bars to the eyes. Note the single line that forms the eyebrow and the nose, and the bar connecting the nose and mouth.

Here the eyes are adjusted by elongating the lids to form the connecting bars.

The eyes have been stylized by elongating them and removing the details of the pupils. The hairline has also been adjusted to connect with the eyebrows.

SIDE VIEW

The lines of both the eye and brow are elongated to form the bars.

The hairline has been changed to form the connecting bars. This technique creates a more realistic appearance in the eyes.

PRACTICE DESIGN. *Based on a poster by Alphonse Mucha (1860–1939).*

CHAPTER 7

THE FLYING HORSE OF KANSU, *a traditional old image familiar throughout Asia.*

Enlarging and Reducing Designs

In copying, it is not always possible to find a picture or design in exactly the right size you may wish to use; the design may be too small or too large. The very simple method explained here will allow you to change the size of any image to suit your purposes. To enlarge a picture, follow the steps listed below; reducing is a similar process, as explained in step 10. You will use the same basic materials for this procedure as you did in previous chapters.

PROCEDURE

1. Choose a picture or design, such as the example shown here, that you wish to enlarge.
2. Using tracing paper or carbon and typewriter paper, make a clear copy of the picture.
3. With a ruler and a soft-lead pencil, mark the design off in a grid of ¼″ (0.64 cm) squares as shown.
4. Decide on the size you want your picture to be; then, on another sheet of paper, make another grid according to that size. If you want your picture to be double the size of the original, mark your grid in ½″ (1.27 cm) squares; to triple the size, mark off ¾″ (1.91 cm) squares; and to quadruple it, mark off 1″ (2.54 cm) squares.
5. Copy the contents of each square of the original picture in the corresponding square of the enlarged grid.
6. Make a copy of your enlargement without the grid on a clean piece of white paper using carbon or tracing paper.
7. Make whatever adjustments are necessary; add connecting bars where needed.
8. Following the steps you learned in the previous chapters, make the final cutout.
9. Complete the additional practice designs.
10. *To reduce a design:* Merely transfer the image from a large grid to a smaller one. For example, to reduce an image by half, draw a grid of ½″ (1.27 cm) squares over the original picture and transfer it to a ¼″ (0.64 cm) grid; to reduce the image by a third, use a ¾″ (1.91 cm) grid and transfer to a ¼″ (0.64 cm) grid.

Enlarging a design.

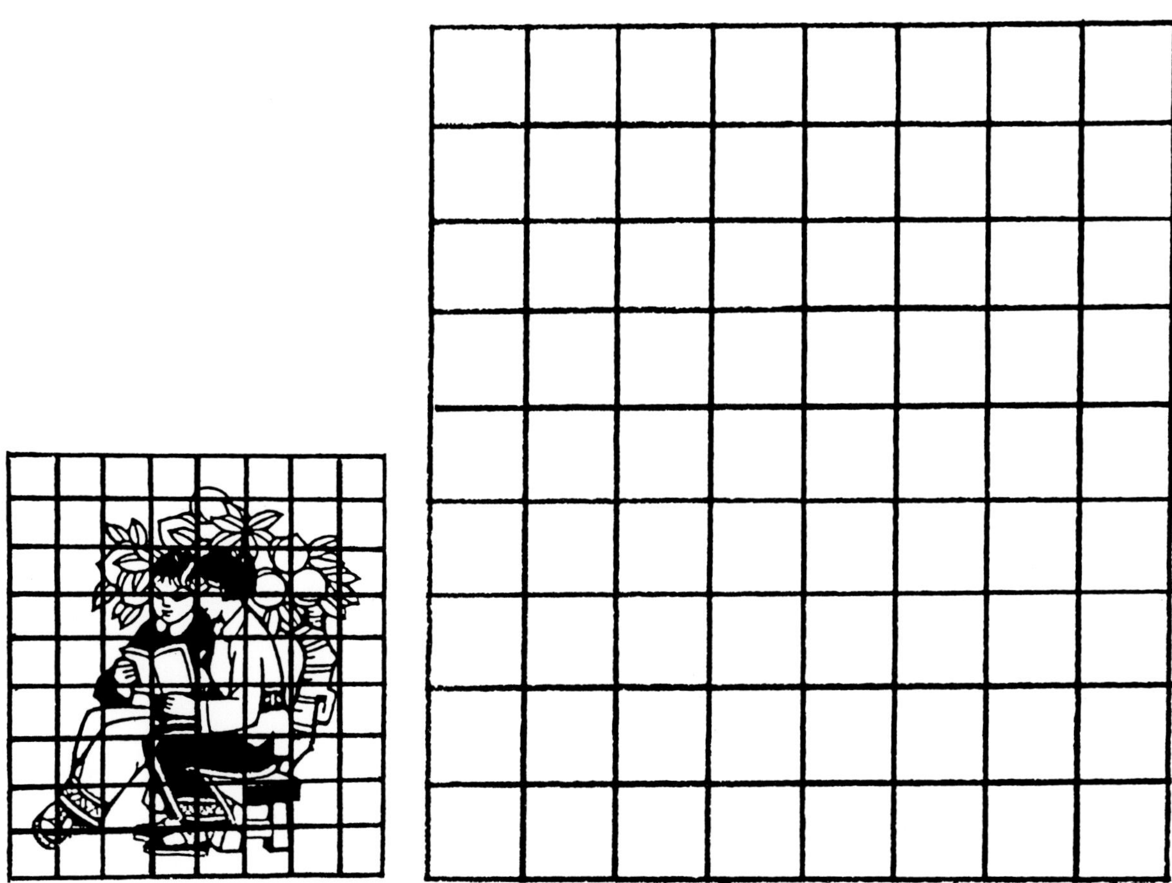

PRACTICE DESIGN

PRACTICE GRID

PRACTICE DESIGN

PRACTICE DESIGN

CHAPTER 8

CHINESE BRIDGE.

Reflections

ALTHOUGH the Western concept of symmetry is not usually considered an acceptable compositional approach in most traditional Asian art, the "reflection" picture, in which the top half of the image is symmetrically repeated as the bottom half as though reflected in a stream or lake, is a time-honored cut-art technique, particularly among the Chinese. It should be noted, however, that the technique creates more of a mirror image than the kind of reflection that would appear in the physical world, where, for example, a ripple on the water's surface would distort the image. In this type of paper-cut the reflection is identical to its subject but inverted. This slight touch of artistic license does not detract from the beauty of the paper-cut in any way.

There are two methods for creating the "reflection" paper-cut, each having certain advantages over the other. I suggest you try both. You will need the same basic materials you used in previous chapters.

PROCEDURE

Method One

The advantage of this method of cutting a reflection is that it is faster than the second; however, the technique does not allow you to depict such details as ripples and waves in the bottom half of the picture, which would give the reflection a more naturalistic appearance.

With this method you will be folding your paper, so use a thinner kind such as origami paper, since heavier types tend to crack and will show the crease in your finished cut.

FIGURE 1

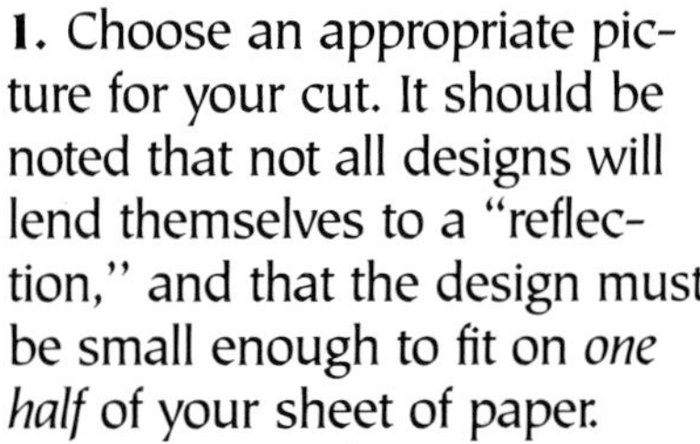

1. Choose an appropriate picture for your cut. It should be noted that not all designs will lend themselves to a "reflection," and that the design must be small enough to fit on *one half* of your sheet of paper.
2. Draw your design on a sheet of white paper as you have done in the previous chapters, but use only the top half of the paper (Figure 1).

FIGURE 2

3. Fold your sheet of colored paper in half (Figure 2); then tape your pattern to the folded paper, with the bottom of your design *exactly* on the fold of the colored paper (Figure 3). So that they will not slip during cutting, make certain that the pattern and the two parts of the folded paper are taped securely together.
4. With a *very* sharp blade, cut out the design as you have done in previous projects, making certain that you cut through the pattern and both halves of the sheet of colored paper.
5. When the design has been cut out completely, carefully remove the pattern, and unfold your finished "reflection."

FIGURE 3

PRACTICE DESIGNS

PROCEDURE

Method Two

Although this method has the disadvantage of taking twice as long to complete as the first, it does allow you to add ripples and waves (the Chinese sometimes even add fish), which will give a truer feeling of a reflection in water. And because you do not fold the colored paper, this method works better on heavier types that might otherwise show a crease in the finished cut.

1. Choose an appropriate picture as you did for the first method.
2. Draw your design on one half of a sheet of white paper, just as in the first method.
3. Take a second sheet of white paper and fold it in half.
4. Cut a sheet of carbon paper in half.
5. Place your half-sheet design on *top* of the upper half of the folded white sheet so that the bottom of the design is *exactly* on the fold of the full sheet.
6. Slip a half sheet of carbon paper, *carbon side down*, between the design and the top of the folded white sheet (Figure 1).
7. Place the other half sheet of carbon paper, *carbon side up*, under the bottom half of the folded white paper (Figure 1).
8. Tape the sheets securely together.
9. With a sharp pencil or a ball-point pen, trace your design, pressing heavily with the pencil or pen so that the design will be transferred clearly to both halves of the folded white sheet.
10. Remove the pattern, and unfold the full sheet of white paper. Your design should now appear on the upper half of the full sheet, with the inverted reflection on the bottom half.
11. If the reflection is a bit faint, go over it with a pencil or a felt-tip pen.
12. On the bottom half of the picture draw in ripples, waves, fish—whatever will give a more natural appearance to the reflection (Figure 2, opposite).
13. Tape your pattern (the full white sheet) to a sheet of colored paper, and cut out the design as you have done in previous projects.
14. Complete the additional practice designs.

FIGURE 1

FIGURE 2

PRACTICE DESIGN. *Try both methods with this and the designs on page 51.*

CHAPTER 9

Mounting Cut-Art

HAVING NOW PRACTICED the basic techniques of cut-art, you should have a number of completed paper-cuts filed away. A work of art can never be fully appreciated, however, if it is merely tucked inside a folder and hidden from view. To enjoy the results of your long hours of effort, you will certainly want to mount some works for display. Also, most of the paper-cuts made using the advanced techniques that follow this chapter require mounting, so it is important that you practice the methods introduced here. I should indicate that these methods are those that, after much experimentation, have proved most useful for me. As you gain more expertise in cut-art, you will discover the working methods that suit you best.

As you look over your completed cuts, you may find that because of the amount of detail involved or the thinness of the paper, some are too delicate and fragile to permit much handling. For proper care, such cuts should be framed behind glass (see Chapter 20, Framing and Displaying Cut-Art). Mounting them according to method 1 explained below involves minimal handling. Other types of cuts, including the special Japanese formats of *tanzaku* and *shikishi* (explained in Chapter 20), require mounting method 2 or 3, described here.

MATERIALS

Depending on which method you use, you will need:

- Completed paper-cuts
- Mounting board of appropriate size
- Ruler
- Soft-lead pencil
- Wax paper
- Fine-tip paintbrush
- Rubber cement and water-soluble white glue
- White typewriter paper
- Brayer (optional)
- Art-gum or pencil-shaped typewriter eraser
- Vinyl or acetate folders (optional)

Paper-cuts are best displayed on white, 4- to 10-ply mounting board; however, other light, pastel colors may be used if desired. If you plan to frame your pictures, you can save some expense by mounting them on board that will fit standard-size frames — 5 × 7″ (12.7 × 17.8 cm), 8 × 10″ (20.3 × 25.4 cm), and so on. For *shikishi*, use mounting board that measures 9½ × 10¼″ (24.1 × 26.0 cm); for *tanzaku*, use 2⅜ × 14¼″ (6.03 × 36.2 cm) board.

Once your cut has been firmly mounted, you may wish to give it a protective coating with an artist's fixative, a clear acrylic spray available at most craft and art shops in aerosol cans. It gives your picture a transparent shield that guards against stains, smudges, and dust, and also helps to retard fading of some colored papers. There are several kinds on the market, so be sure to read and follow the manufacturer's instructions, which vary from brand to brand.

Method One

This method should be used for cuts that will be framed behind glass — particularly those that require careful handling. The optional method that follows may be used for small pictures, up to 8 × 10″ (20.3 × 25.4 cm). The basic difference is that the picture is mounted inside an acetate or vinyl folder rather than directly to the mounting board.

PROCEDURE

1. Choose an appropriate size mounting board for your cut. It should be large enough to allow for empty space between the edge of the picture and the frame. For example, an 8 × 10″ (20.3 × 25.4 cm) picture should be mounted on either 9 × 12″ or 11 × 14″ (22.9 × 30.5 cm or 27.9 × 35.6 cm) board. (This rule does not apply to the *tanzaku* or *shikishi*; see above and Chapter 20.)
2. Place the picture face up on the mounting board.
3. Measuring with your ruler, center the picture.
4. With a soft-lead pencil, make several light register marks on the mounting board around the outside of the picture as a guide to the cut's final placement.
5. Place the picture *face down* on a sheet of wax paper.
6. With a fine-tip paintbrush, place several small dots of rubber cement or water-soluble white glue on the back of the picture, making certain that the adhesive is not applied so thickly that it runs. The purpose of these dots of glue is merely to hold the picture to the mounting board so that it does not slip once it is framed. A few dots at strategic points — such as the corners or the edges — should be sufficient.
7. Lift the picture carefully, turn it face up, and place it on the mounting board inside the penciled register marks.
8. Place a sheet of clean white typewriter paper over the picture and press down gently with your palm or roll with a brayer. Then carefully remove the typewriter paper.
9. With an eraser, gently erase the register marks.
10. Clean your brush.
11. For framing instructions, see Chapter 20, Framing and Displaying Cut-Art.

Optional Procedure

1. Obtain a mounting board that measures 8 × 10″ (20.3 × 25.4 cm).
2. Cut an acetate or vinyl folder (the kind of protector you have been using to file your cutouts) to measure 8 × 10″ (20.3 × 25.4 cm). Cut on the sides *opposite* the fold so that the folder remains in one piece.
3. Follow steps 2–6 of the procedure outlined above. In step 6, however, you will need only one or two dots of adhesive along the top edge of the picture.
4. Place the vinyl folder on top of the mounting board so that they align, and open the folder. The register marks should show through the vinyl.
5. Following steps 7 and 8 above, carefully glue the picture *inside* the vinyl folder that covers the mounting board (see illustration).
6. Place the other half of the vinyl folder over the picture, which is now *between* the protective sheets.
7. Follow steps 9–11 above. The mounting board is placed behind the vinyl folder when you frame a picture mounted this way.

Method Two

This method should be used only for *monochrome* paper-cuts that must be firmly and completely glued to the mounting board.

PROCEDURE

1. Follow steps 1–4 of the procedure for method 1, making certain that the register marks are dark enough to be seen through a sheet of wax paper.
2. Cut a sheet of wax paper slightly larger than your picture.
3. Place the picture face down on the wax paper.
4. Cover the entire back of the picture with rubber cement. *Note*: In this method, rubber cement only should be used.
5. Lift the wax paper on which your picture lies and turn it over so that the glued side of the picture is toward the mounting board. The excess rubber cement around the edges of the cut will hold it in place.
6. Place the wax paper on the mounting board so that the picture is aligned within the register marks.
7. Gently press down on the wax paper with the palm of your hand, or gently roll it with a brayer.
8. Carefully peel the wax paper away from the picture.
9. Cover the picture with a sheet of clean white paper and press down again. Carefully remove this paper.
10. Check all the lines of your cut to make certain that they are all firmly cemented to the mounting board. Any section of the picture that does not adhere should be carefully lifted with the flat side of your cutting blade so you can apply additional rubber cement underneath with a fine-tip brush. Press down on that section until it is securely in place.
11. To remove the excess rubber cement that is now on the face of your picture, go over it carefully with an art-gum or pencil-shaped typewriter eraser. *Do not* use a pink or other color eraser, which may leave marks on your mounting board. I personally prefer the pencil-shaped kind because it gets into the smaller cuts more easily than an art-gum eraser. Whichever type you use, *rub gently!*
12. Complete steps 9–11 of the procedure for method 1.

Method Three

This method of mounting is a bit more difficult than the others and requires some practice. It is, however, the only one I have found that works well for advanced-technique cuts. I suggest you try it first on something simple, something you have not put a lot of time and effort into. *Note*: Any of the spray adhesives now on the market can also be used with method 3. They do require a bit more deftness and care than rubber cement or white glue, but are well worth experimenting with.

PROCEDURE

1. Follow steps 1–5 of the procedure explained in method 1.
2. With a fine-tip brush, apply a thin coat of rubber cement or water-soluble white glue diluted with a few drops of boiling water to the *right half* of the face-down cut. This must be done carefully so that glue does not get on the front of the picture.
3. Gently lift the picture, turn it over, and carefully and accurately place it within the register marks. Press down. The left half of your picture should now be firmly attached to the mounting board.
4. Lift the right half (the unglued portion) of your picture and pull it back from the mounting board with your left hand. With the right hand, slide a clean piece of wax paper between the picture and the mounting board, moving it far enough to the left so it comes to rest against the glued portion of your picture. The wax paper protects the mounting board during the next step.
5. Still holding the unglued portion of the picture in your left hand, apply a thin coat of adhesive to cover that part.
6. Remove the wax paper and carefully lower the remainder of the picture to the mounting board.
7. Cover the picture with a sheet of clean white paper and gently press down on it with your palm or roll it with a brayer.
8. Complete steps 10–11 of the procedure for method 1.

PART TWO

ADVANCED TECHNIQUES: APPLIQUE AND PAINTED PAPER-CUTS

CHAPTER 10

ON THE INLAND SEA, JAPAN.

One-Color Appliqué

THE SIMPLEST and quickest method for appliquéing color to a paper-cut is to glue a piece of colored paper to your mounting board, then mount the cut over it. This elementary approach does have its limitations, working well only for those cuts that do not require a diversity of color. It is most effective with cuts that are more silhouettelike in nature.

Almost any color and kind of paper can be used for this technique. I personally prefer tissue paper. It is a bit more fragile to handle than heavier types like construction paper, but it comes in a wide range of shades and adds a richness of color that most other papers lack. Variegated tissue papers are especially beautiful, and are more versatile than the regular one-color papers. I highly recommend their use wherever possible.

MATERIALS

- Completed paper-cut to be mounted
- Mounting board
- Colored paper for background
- Ruler
- Soft-lead pencil
- Scissors
- Rubber cement or water-soluble white glue
- Fine-tip brushes
- White typewriter paper
- Brayer (optional)

PROCEDURE

1. Choose a mounting board appropriate to the size of your cut (see step 1, method 1 in Chapter 9, Mounting Cut-Art).
2. Choose a background paper that will establish the mood you want in the finished picture.
3. Place the cut face up on the mounting board.
4. Measuring with your ruler, center the picture.
5. With a soft-lead pencil, make several light register marks on the mounting board around the outside of the picture. These will guide you in the final placement of the cut.
6. Trim your background paper slightly smaller than the cut so that no color will show beyond the border when the cut is in place.
7. Beginning at the top register mark on the mounting board, apply a *thin* coating of rubber cement or water-soluble white glue thinned with a few drops of boiling water. Do not cover the entire area to be glued;

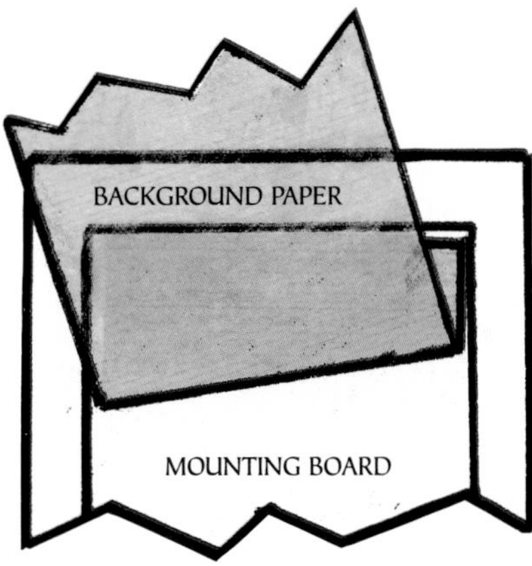

rather, apply the adhesive in a strip about 2″ (5.1 cm) wide, then place the top edge of the background paper slightly inside the top register mark (see illustration above). Press the background paper firmly to the mounting board with your hand. Lift the unglued section of the background paper with

CHOOSING THE RIGHT BACKGROUND COLOR

The color you choose as a background for your cut should enhance the mood of your finished picture. For example, for a morning mood try light pinks, blues, greens, or yellows; for midday, a darker blue, darker yellow, or light orange would be appropriate; for sunset or twilight, lavenders, light reds, and darker pinks and oranges are effective; and for nighttime, use deeper blues or greens. Experiment with several colors—especially with variegated tissues—before you decide on the final one.

A note of caution: Be sure your background color is not so dark that your cut is lost. If you wish to use a dark background, however, you can achieve an interesting effect by using a "double cut" (see illustration below). In this technique you make two cuts at the same time, one black and one white. The white cut is mounted first, then the black one is positioned over but slightly below it to create a highlight.

your left hand and, with the right hand, apply glue to the next 2″ (5.1 cm) section of the mounting board. Repeat this process until the entire sheet of background paper is firmly glued to the mounting board.

8. Cover the glued background paper with a sheet of white paper and press down firmly on the overall surface with your hand, or roll it with a brayer.

9. If you use diluted white glue on a lightweight mounting board, you may find that the board has a tendency to curl. If this happens, before you mount the cut, place the mounting board on a smooth surface and cover it with a heavy book. Leave it under this weight overnight before applying the cut.

10. Once the background color is in place, mount your cut using method 3 in Chapter 9, Mounting Cut-Art.

11. Should your mounting board curl after the cut has been applied, press it under a heavy book once again.

PRACTICE DESIGN

CHAPTER 11

Two-Color Cut-Art

IN CERTAIN PARTS of China, two-color paper-cuts are very popular and have reached a high level of artistic craftsmanship. Cuts from Hailun County, Heilongjiang Province, are particularly elaborate and exquisitely detailed; simpler designs found elsewhere are no less delightful and strikingly beautiful.

In this technique, the design is cut from two different colored papers and then glued together to form the final picture, as in the simplified example shown here.

You will need the same basic materials for this project as you did in the section on monochrome cut-art, including two sheets of colored paper, one black and one of a contrasting color.

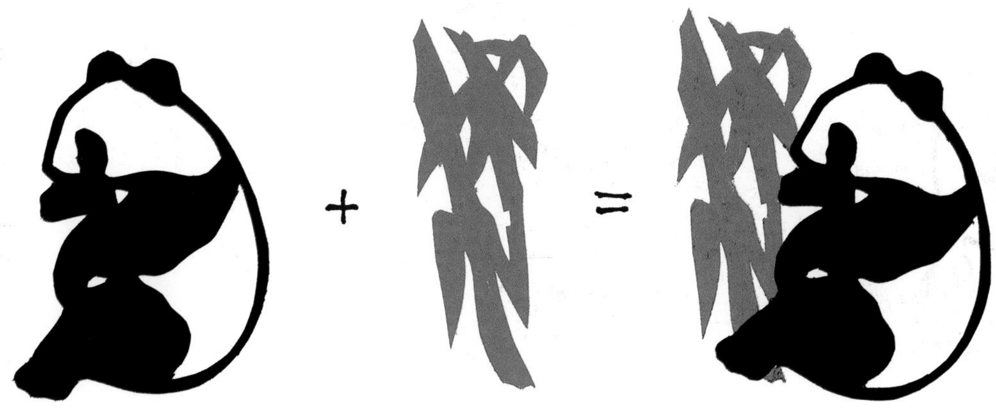

PROCEDURE

1. Make a preliminary sketch of your design, indicating which part will be done in black and which will be done in the contrasting color (Figure 1). Note that in the final product, the black cut will be mounted over the contrasting one.

2. Using tracing paper or carbon and typewriter paper, make two patterns, one for the black paper and one for the contrasting color (Figures 2 and 3).

3. Tape one pattern to the black paper, the other to the contrasting sheet. Cut out the designs as you did the monochrome paper-cuts.

4. Place the black design on top of the contrasting one to make certain that they fit together as intended; trim any colored areas that should not be exposed.

5. Choose an appropriate mounting board (see Chapter 9, Mounting Cut-Art).

6. Using either mounting method 2 or 3 (Chapter 9), glue your contrasting design to the mounting board (Figure 4).

7. Using mounting method 3 (Chapter 9), glue the black design carefully on top of the contrasting design (Figure 5).

8. If there are still places where the two designs do not fit exactly—particularly along the outside edges—carefully trim them with your cutting knife.

9. *Note*: In the first practice design, you have already been given the patterns for the two colors so that you can practice cutting and gluing. In the additional designs, you will need to decide which portion of each will be black and which will be the contrasting color.

FIGURE 1

FIGURE 2

FIGURE 3

FIGURE 4

FIGURE 5

PRACTICE DESIGN

PRACTICE DESIGN

PRACTICE DESIGN

CHAPTER 12

Partial Appliqué

IN JAPAN *kiri-e* artists use a technique similar to the two-color paper-cuts of China to add colorful highlights to their work. The important point to note here is *highlight,* because color is applied only to certain areas. Colored highlights are usually glued to the mounting board before the cut itself is attached, but in the illustration shown opposite, highlights have been added both behind and on top of the cut.

An irregularly shaped piece of pink paper placed behind the branches of a cherry tree brings the color of the blossoms to life. A piece of blue paper appropriately placed suddenly focuses our attention on a shadow; a piece of yellow paper becomes moonlight reflecting on water, allowing the imagination, as in so much Japanese art, to complete the remainder of the picture. The important thing to remember is that you are merely highlighting a specific aspect of the picture, not coloring the entire image.

In addition to the basic materials you have used in the previous chapters, you will need several different colors of paper, depending on the highlights you plan to add to your cut.

PROCEDURE

FIGURE 1

FIGURE 2

FIGURE 3

1. Make a monochrome papercut (Figure 1).
2. Place the cut on an appropriate mounting board, and make your register marks (see Chapter 9). Holding the cut firmly in place with one hand, make a light pencil tracing of it (Figure 2) as a guide for the proper placement of color highlights.
3. Decide which sections of the cut you want to highlight and which colors you will use. You may find it helpful to place your cut on several different sheets of colored paper to determine this.
4. Lightly trace your monochrome cut onto the colored paper. Cut out the appropriate shapes, making them *slightly* larger than the outlines, and glue them to the mounting board (Figure 3).
5. Using mounting method 3 (Chapter 9), carefully glue your cut to the mounting board (Figure 4).
6. Complete the practice design.

FIGURE 4

PRACTICE DESIGN

CHAPTER 13

Full-Color Appliqué: Direct Method

IN FULL-COLOR appliqué, the paper-cut artist applies various colors of paper to a picture just as a painter would use oil or watercolor. There are two basic approaches to this technique, and for lack of a better name, I call the first method "direct appliqué," because the colors are applied directly to the back of the paper-cut itself before it is mounted. A wide range of different types of colored paper will work well and may be used together to create interesting texture variations.

MATERIALS

In addition to the materials you used in previous chapters, you will need:

Origami, construction, gift, and tissue papers

Wax paper

Tweezers

Eraser

Gold or copper foil or gift wrap (optional)

PROCEDURE

FIGURE 1

FIGURE 2

FIGURE 3

1. Make a monochrome paper-cut as you did in previous projects (Figure 1).

2. Decide what colors you will need for the picture, giving consideration to the variations needed for shadows, highlights, and so on. For example, you may need two or more shades of green for a tree or a grove of trees, since trees in nature are not a uniform color. The same applies if you are showing a mountain range receding toward the horizon; the mountains in the foreground will be darker than those in the distance.

3. Once you have decided on which colors to use, you can begin applying them to each separate section of the picture.

4. Place a piece of tracing paper over the section to which color is to be applied. With a soft-lead pencil, carefully trace the outline of that section on the tracing paper to make a pattern (Figure 2).

5. Cut the pattern from the tracing paper. Place it on the colored paper you have chosen for that section and outline it (Figure 3). Then carefully cut out the colored-paper shape (Figure 4). *Note*: If you are using tissue paper for the color appliqué, you can eliminate the tracing paper and trace the pattern directly onto the transparent tissue.

6. Place your paper-cut *face down* on a piece of clean wax paper, and apply a coat of rubber cement to the section of the paper-cut where color is to be applied.

7. Carefully lift your cut from the wax paper and, still keeping it face down, place it on another sheet of clean wax paper.

8. With a pair of tweezers, carefully place the colored-paper pattern on the glued section of the cut (Figure 5). If the appliqué does not fit exactly, peel it from the paper-cut, trim it where necessary, and replace it. I recommend rubber cement here because it allows you to remove and replace sections easily without tearing the paper-cut.

9. With an eraser or your finger, rub off any excess rubber cement before you turn the cut over. This is very important, because if it is not removed, it will form lumps and cause problems later when the picture is to be mounted. Also, removing the excess cement reduces the possibility of your fingers sticking to the picture and tearing it. When your picture is finished, the back should be clean of cement.

10. Gently lift your cut and turn it face up. With an eraser, carefully remove any rubber cement that has come through to the front of the picture. I emphasize *carefully*, because too much pressure will tear tissue paper, fray construction paper, and remove the color from origami paper. Rubber cement that is not removed will eventually turn brown.

11. Check to see that the color appliqué is fully cemented to the cut. If it is not, use your small brush to reglue the loose sections.

12. Rub the rubber cement off both pieces of wax paper before you proceed to apply color to the next section.

13. Follow steps 4–12 with each section of the cut until you have applied all the color (Figure 6).

14. Choose an appropriate size mounting board (see Chapter 9, Mounting Cut-Art). To mount a full-color direct appliqué, follow the procedure outlined in Chapter 10, One-Color Appliqué, but omit the application of background paper.

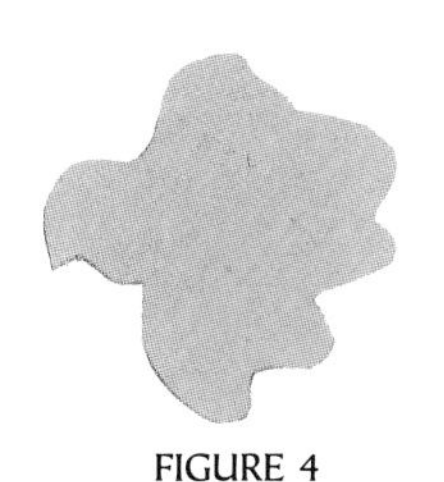

FIGURE 4

FIGURE 5

FIGURE 6

PRACTICE DESIGN

The Chinese create particularly elegant paper-cuts using very thin gold or copper foil; gold gift wrap makes an excellent substitute. This figure is shown in the traditional costume of the Japanese Peacock Dance.

PRACTICE DESIGN. *Try this one in gold paper.*

CHAPTER 14

Full-Color Appliqué: Overlay Method

THE SECOND METHOD of full-color appliqué is a bit more difficult than the first, requiring more of an artist's eye and imagination. With a little practice, however, even a beginner can soon achieve pleasing results.

The techniques of the overlay appliqué method are drawn from both collage (Example 1, next page), a Western art form first created by Picasso and his contemporary Georges Braque around 1912; and *chigiri-e* (Example 2, next page), a Japanese art form created by the nobility more than 800 years ago. Both approaches use bits and pieces of paper that are glued to a background to form a design or picture; the difference between them is that in collage the paper is usually *cut,* while in *chigiri-e* it is usually *torn.* This distinction may seem trivial, but if you study the examples shown here, the effects unique to each approach will become apparent.

In *kiri-e* the artist cuts or tears the colors for the background and applies them directly to the mounting board, as in partial-color appliqué. Then the paper-cut is glued over the background colors. For this reason, I call it the overlay method.

Overlay is more difficult than direct appliqué because, with the exception of a few broad guidelines, there is no single, specific procedure for applying

MATERIALS

In addition to the materials you used in the previous chapter, you will need:

Water-soluble white glue

Watercolor paints or colored pencils

the background color. The method you use and the order in which you apply the colors will vary from picture to picture. This calls for a bit more creativity and skill than did previous projects. Therefore, it should be noted that the procedure outlined in this chapter is a rather general one that will need to be modified according to the final effect you wish to achieve in each individual picture.

Before we begin, let us take note of the guidelines I mentioned above. These apply to all full-color cuts made using the overlay method:

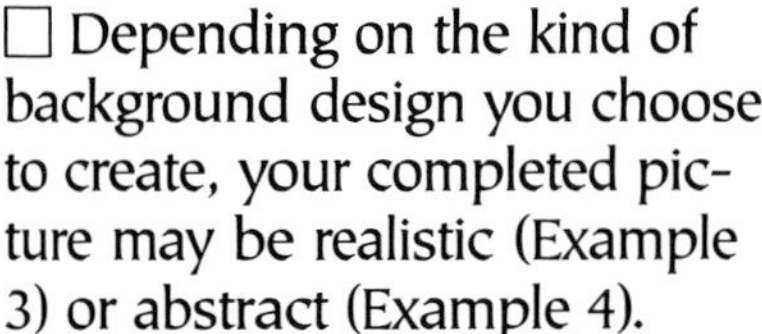

☐ Depending on the kind of background design you choose to create, your completed picture may be realistic (Example 3) or abstract (Example 4).

☐ When you are creating mountains, water, earth, sky, shadows, and the like, colors may be glued directly one over another.

☐ In creating such elements as shadows or clouds, where a soft, diffused edge is desirable in the overlay, the paper should be torn rather than cut. To tear, draw the pattern on the paper with a wet fine-tip brush and gently pull away along the moistened line.

☐ Colors in tissue paper and some construction papers may bleed when wet; therefore, glue should be applied to the mounting board rather than to the colored paper.

☐ For best results in gluing, use water-soluble white glue diluted with an equal amount of warm water. Rubber cement does not work very well here, particularly on torn paper.

EXAMPLE 1: *Collage,* LADY KASA LISTENING TO THE BELLS.

EXAMPLE 2: *Chigiri-e,* SAKURA TO FUJI-SAN.

EXAMPLE 3: *Realistic.*

EXAMPLE 4: *Abstract.*

PROCEDURE

1. To study shading and color values, I find it helpful to first make a rough sketch of the design and color it with either watercolors or colored pencils (Figure 1). This will be used later as a guide for applying the colored paper to the mounting board.
2. Cover the rough sketch with a piece of tracing paper. Draw the pattern for the paper-cut (Figure 2).
3. Make your monochrome paper-cut as you did in previous projects (Figure 3, over).
4. Lightly trace the design onto the mounting board to use as a guideline for the appliqué.
5. Place a piece of tracing paper over the paper-cut, and trace the pattern for the sky (Figure 4, over; the area to be traced is shown here in red).
6. Trace the pattern for the sky onto blue paper. Cut it out and apply it to the mounting board, using diluted water-soluble white glue (Figure 5).
7. Following the same procedure, cut out and mount the green paper for the trees (Figure 6); then cut out and mount brown paper for the rocks and gold foil for the water (Figure 7).
8. Using your color sketch as a guide, cut (or tear) and mount yellow tissue clouds, light green tree highlights, blue shadows on the rocks, and blue tissue on the water (Figure 8).
9. Tear out and mount gray cloud shadows, tree trunks, and purple shadows on the rocks (Figure 9).
10. Using mounting method 3 (Chapter 9), mount the completed monochrome paper-cut to the colored background (Figure 10). You can use rubber cement here.
11. Complete the practice designs. For the first one you have been given both a suggested color scheme (page 86) and the design for the monochrome overlay (page 87). On pages 88 and 89 you have been given only the suggested color schemes, so you will have to follow through all the steps to complete those cuts.

FIGURE 1

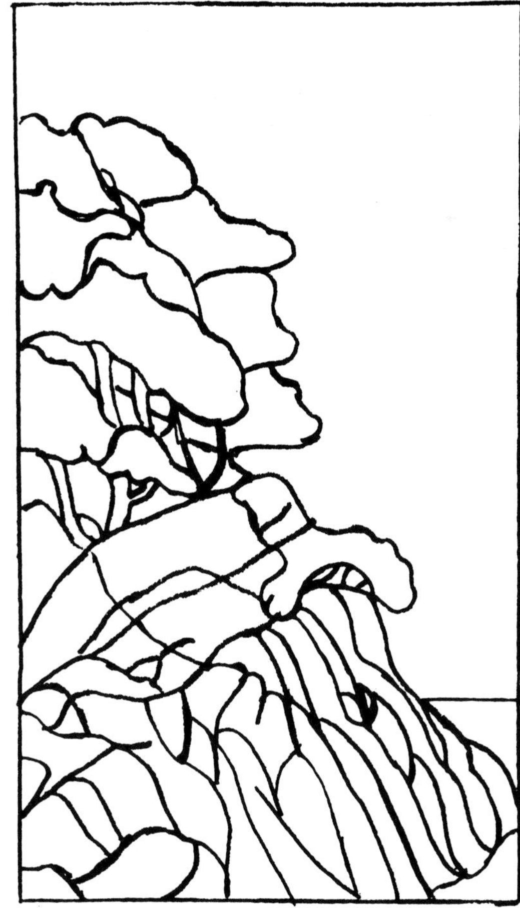
FIGURE 2

FIGURE 3

FIGURE 4

FIGURE 5

FIGURE 6

FIGURE 7

FIGURE 8

FIGURE 9

FIGURE 10

PRACTICE DESIGN *(suggested color scheme).*

Monochrome overlay for practice design opposite.

PRACTICE DESIGN *(suggested color scheme).*

PRACTICE DESIGN *(suggested color scheme).*

CHAPTER 15

Full-Color Painted Paper-Cuts

IN THIS TECHNIQUE the picture is first cut from white paper and is then completely colored with watercolor paints or colored felt-tip pens. The approach outlined here will allow you to create an approximation of the traditional painted paper-cuts of China.

In China's Hebei Province, where this technique was perfected, a stack of paper-cuts is made at one time and is dampened slightly. Dyes are then applied, and because the paper is unsized and therefore rather porous, color permeates the entire stack, creating brightly hued pictures such as this opera mask, a design originated by Wan Lao Shan (1890–1951), a famous artist from Yuxian in Hebei Province. As the dyes filter through the stack of paper, colors placed on top of others to create highlights and shadows have a tendency to fuse, resulting in a very lovely muted effect, as in the peony on page 92.

Although limited to making one picture at a time, we can create very similar and very pleasing effects in our own cuts by using watercolors or felt-tip pens. Japanese *sumi-e* paper, available by mail or in Oriental specialty shops, is excellent for this kind of paper-cut. If you choose colored felt-tip pens you will need a wide range, since it is difficult to blend shades the way you can with watercolors.

MATERIALS

In addition to the materials you have used in previous chapters, you will need:

Heavyweight white drawing paper or *sumi-e* paper

Watercolor paints or felt-tip pens

Chinese opera mask by Wan Lao Shan (1890–1951).

Dyed paper-cut from the People's Republic of China.

PROCEDURE

1. Make a sketch or pattern for your picture. Note, however, this important difference: In earlier monochrome cuts, you have cut out all but the outlining details, as in Figure 1; in this particular project, you should remove less detail so you will have more area on which to apply color, as in Figure 2. Note that in Figure 2 all the *black* areas will be cut out; the white area that remains is the design you will paint.
2. Tape your sketch or pattern to a clean sheet of white drawing paper, and cut out your design as you have done with all previous cuts.
3. Place your cutout face up on a clean sheet of colored paper (Figure 3). This lets you see your design more clearly so you can determine exactly where to apply the paint.
4. Using watercolors or felt-tip pens, first apply the base colors to the picture (Figure 3). If you are using watercolors, be sure to clean your brush carefully before changing hues.
5. Place the cut face up on a clean sheet of white paper to see if your colors are dark enough to show up against a light background. Darken where necessary. Complete your picture by applying shadows to the appropriate areas (Figure 4).
6. Allow the picture to dry thoroughly before handling it. Should it curl, once it is dry place it between two sheets of clean paper and press with a warm iron.
7. Using mounting method 3 (Chapter 9), carefully mount your finished picture on light-colored board.

FIGURE 1

FIGURE 2

FIGURE 3

FIGURE 4

PRACTICE DESIGN *Design adapted from a piece of Chinese embroidery.*

PRACTICE DESIGN. Remember: *The black areas are to be cut away; the white design is the part you will color.*

CHAPTER 16

After a woodcut by Utamaro (1750–1806).

Painted Backgrounds

THERE ARE TWO APPROACHES to applying paint to a background of a paper-cut. In the first method, you mount the cut on a white background, just as you did with all earlier monochrome cuts; then you paint in the color with watercolors or felt-tip pens. This technique is excellent when subtle shadings are desired, and works best with watercolors because you can mix them easily to get a broad range of shades. If you are going to use watercolors, I strongly recommend working with a fine-tip Japanese ink brush, which will give you better control, particularly in the small areas.

In the second method, you color the background first, then mount the paper-cut on top of it. You will need the same materials you used in the last chapter, plus black paper for the monochrome cut.

PROCEDURE

Method One

1. Make a sketch for your cut as you have done in previous projects.
2. To get an idea as to how and where the color will be applied to your final picture, paint your sketch (Figure 1).
3. Make your monochrome cut and mount it on porous white drawing paper—the same kind you used for your cut in Chapter 15 (Figure 2).
4. Apply the base color to the background (Figure 3).
5. Add and blend the other colors (Figure 4).

USING THE BRUSH

You will have greater control over your brush if you hold it as Chinese and Japanese artists do: vertically, with the little finger resting on the paper for balance and firm support.

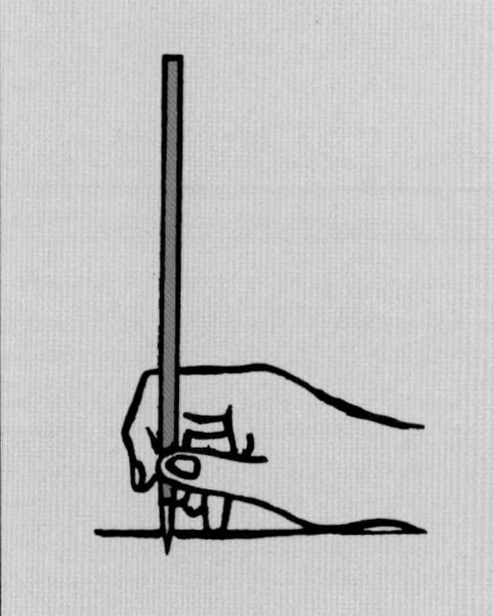

FIGURE 1

FIGURE 2

FIGURE 3

FIGURE 4

PRACTICE DESIGNS

PROCEDURE

Method Two

1. Make the monochrome cut as you have done in previous projects (Figure 1).
2. Place the cut on a piece of white paper and, with a pencil, draw a faint outline of it. I have deliberately drawn the lines darker here to show this point more clearly (Figure 2).
3. Using watercolors or felt-tip pens, color in and blend the background (Figure 3).
4. Carefully mount the cut to the painted background (Figure 4).

FIGURE 1

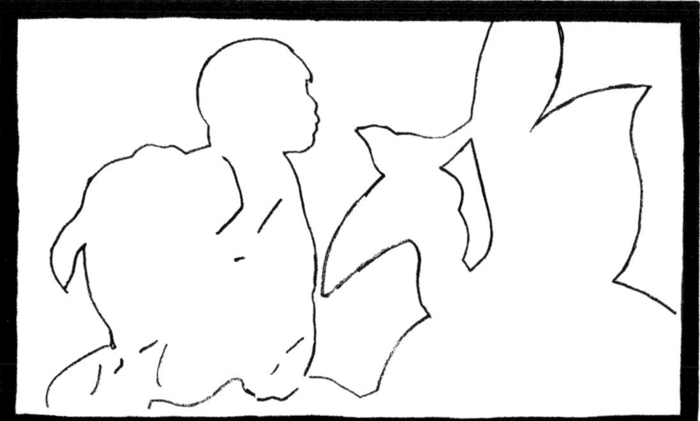

FIGURE 2

FIGURE 3

FIGURE 4

PRACTICE DESIGN

PRACTICE DESIGN *After a woodcut by Kiyomasu (active 1690s–1720s).*

PRACTICE DESIGN

CHAPTER 17

Spatter-Painted Backgrounds

I AM CERTAIN there are very few people who, in their early elementary school days, did not make at least one picture by brushing paint through a mesh screen to create a spattered design on a piece of paper. Basically the technique is very simple, but Japanese artists have developed—and are still developing—variations that make it possible to add fascinating nuances of color to the traditional paper-cut.

As with some of the earlier projects, the procedure will vary from picture to picture, according to the effect you wish to achieve. There are, of course, certain basic principles upon which all variations are built, and it is with these that we shall be concerned in this and the next two chapters. Once you see how the process works, your own creativity should suggest variations for further experimentation. I personally feel that this technique is the most exciting because of the freedom it allows for exploration.

You will need a screen with a fairly open mesh; I recommend nylon (the kind used for window screens), as it does not rust the way wire mesh does. Bind the edges with masking or plastic tape to prevent poking yourself with protruding wires and to keep the mesh from coming apart.

MATERIALS

In addition to the basic materials you have used in previous projects, you will need:

Absorbent white and colored construction papers for backgrounds

Stiff-bristle brush such as a toothbrush

Watercolors or tempera paints (felt-tip pens won't work)

6 × 6″ (15.2 × 15.2 cm) piece of mesh screen

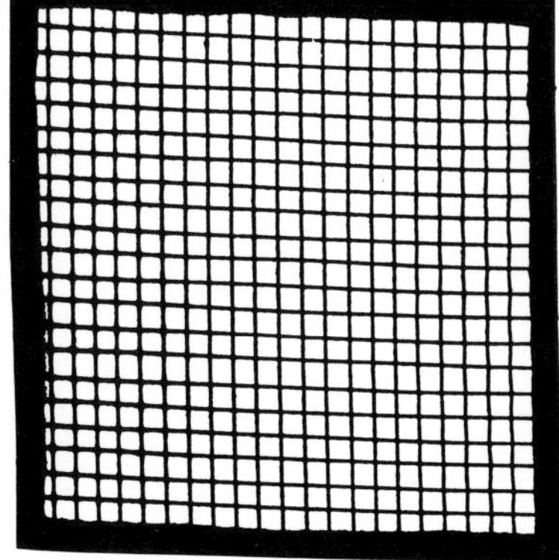

Use a screen with a mesh about this size.

PROCEDURE 1

FIGURE 1

FIGURE 2

The easiest, most basic spatter-painting technique lets you create an overall, one-color background.

1. Make a monochrome cut as you have done in previous projects.

2. Decide on the color of your background paper and paint. I strongly suggest that you experiment with various color combinations before you make your final decision. Not only will this give you a better idea as to what your finished picture will look like, but also it will give you practice in using the brush and screen.

3. Place your background paper on a sheet of newspaper to protect surrounding areas from being spattered with paint.

4. To apply color to the background paper, dip the brush in the paint and brush it over the screen. *Caution:* Do not load your brush with too much paint, or it will collect in blobs on the screen and fall onto your paper. Hold the screen several inches above the paper and move the brush vigorously back and forth across it. You can change the density of the spattered color by applying several coats of paint.

5. Cover the entire background with the spattered paint (Figure 1).

6. Allow the paint to dry completely before handling the paper.

7. Should the paper curl during the drying process, press it under a weight such as a heavy book when it is dry. It may also be pressed with a warm iron. Be sure to press on the unpainted, rather than the painted, side.

8. Carefully apply the monochrome cut to the painted background (Figure 2).

9. Mount the completed picture on heavy poster board.

10. Clean your brush and screen, and make certain that the screen is completely dry, especially if you are using one made of wire instead of nylon.

PROCEDURE 2

When you want to vary a background, you can spatter paint selectively to highlight specific sections of the papercut. The technique involved here is only slightly different from that in procedure 1.

1. Make your monochrome cut.

2. Decide which area of the cut is to be highlighted.

3. Choose your background paper and the color of your paint as you did for procedure 1.

4. Cut out a mask (Figure 1) to cover the portion of the background paper where you do *not* want any color.

5. Position the mask on the background paper, and spatter paint on the uncovered section just as you did in step 4 of procedure 1.

6. Allow the paint to dry completely; then remove the mask (Figure 2).

7. Flatten your background paper as you did in procedure 1.

8. Carefully apply the monochrome cut to the painted background (Figure 3).

9. Mount the completed picture on heavy poster board.

10. Clean and dry your screen and brush. This procedure should be followed each time you use these items.

FIGURE 1

FIGURE 2

FIGURE 3

PROCEDURE 3

This is similar to procedure 2 except that here you use masks to apply two colors to separate portions of the background.

1. Make your monochrome cut.
2. Decide which section of your background will be painted one color and which will be painted the other, as I have done in the example shown here, distinguishing the sky from the water.
3. Choose your background paper and paint colors.
4. As you did in procedure 2, cut out a mask to cover the portion of your background that will be painted the *second* color.
5. Position the mask on the background paper and apply the first color of spattered paint, using the same technique you used in procedures 1 and 2 (Figure 1).
6. Allow the paint to dry completely; then remove the mask.
7. Clean your brush and screen. (Always do this before applying another color.)
8. Cut a second mask to cover the *painted* portion of your background; put it in place and apply your second color (Figure 2).
9. Allow the paint to dry; then remove the second mask (Figure 3).
10. If the background paper curls, flatten it as you did in procedure 1.
11. Carefully apply the monochrome cut to the painted background (Figure 4).
12. Mount the completed picture on heavy poster board.
13. Clean your brush and screen.

FIGURE 1

FIGURE 2

FIGURE 3

FIGURE 4

PROCEDURE 4

Once you master the spatter technique, it is not necessary to stay with backgrounds of one color or of two colors separated by strict boundaries; colors may also be shaded so that one hue overlaps and fades into another. Also, when you mask certain elements of a design—a mountain, a tree, a building—and spatter paint over them, you can add an extra atmospheric dimension to the paper-cut. You can add as many colors to your background as you wish if you remember to mask out all necessary areas each time you spatter on a different hue.

1. As you create the pattern for your paper-cut, decide which part of the design will be created by spattered paint. (Note the mountain in the example shown here.)
2. Make your monochrome cut.
3. Choose your background paper and paint colors.
4. Cut out a mask to cover the portion of the background that will not be painted (Figure 1).
5. Position the mask on the background paper, and spatter on the first color of paint using the same technique as in procedures 1 and 2 (Figure 2). Notice, however, that the color is not applied evenly to the background but is darker at the top and fades out at about the middle of the picture.
6. Leave the mask in place and allow the paint to dry completely.
7. Clean your brush and screen.
8. With the mask still in position, apply the second color (Figure 3). Notice here that the color is darker at the bottom and fades into the first hue in the middle of the picture.
9. Allow the paint to dry; then remove the mask (Figure 4).
10. If the background paper curls, flatten it as you did in the previous procedures.
11. Carefully apply the monochrome cut to the painted background (Figure 5, over).
12. Mount the completed picture on heavy poster board.
13. Clean your brush and screen.

FIGURE 1

FIGURE 2

FIGURE 3

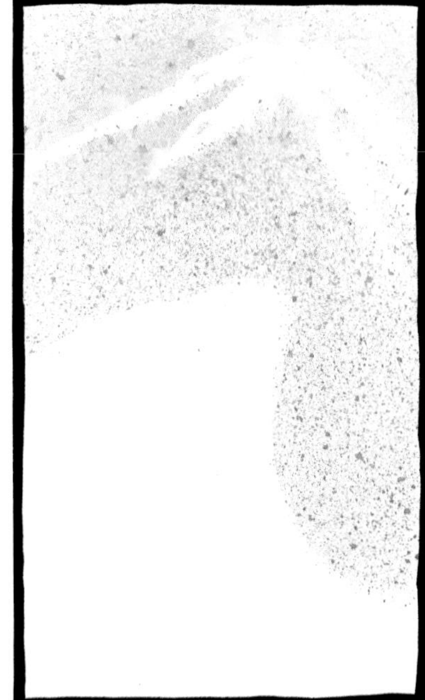

FIGURE 4

FIGURE 5

PRACTICE DESIGN

This is the mask to be used with the practice design on the facing page.

PRACTICE DESIGN

CHAPTER 18

IZANAGI AND IZANAMI ON THE FLOATING BRIDGE OF HEAVEN.

Spatter-Painted Appliqué

SPATTER-PAINTED paper can be appliquéd to a paper-cut the same way you did in Chapter 13 with plain-colored paper. Its advantage is a greater variation in color and texture. For even more variety, you can combine spatter-painted and plain-colored papers in the same paper-cut. You will need the same materials you have used in the previous spatter-painted projects.

PROCEDURE

1. Make your monochrome cut.
2. Prepare a spatter-painted sheet for each color you are going to appliqué (Figures 1–3).
3. Prepare your spatter-painted background as you did in the previous chapter (Figure 4).
4. Appliqué the individual colors to the paper-cut as you did in Chapter 13.
5. Mount the paper-cut on the spatter-painted background (Figure 5).

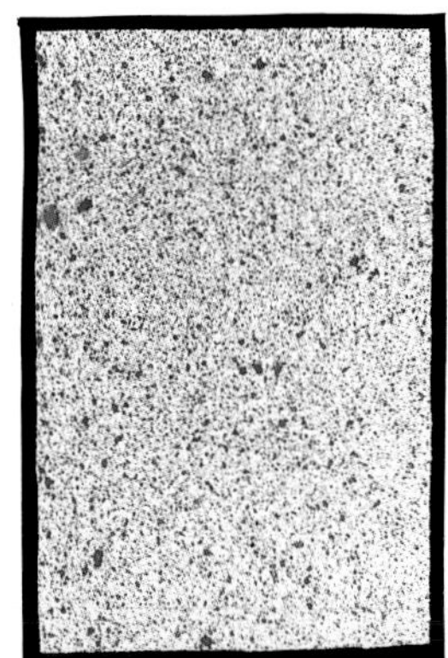

FIGURE 1

FIGURE 2

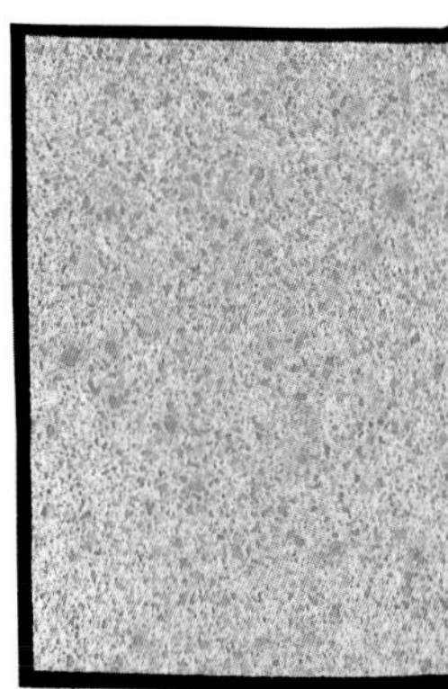

FIGURE 3

FIGURE 5

FIGURE 4

PRACTICE DESIGN. *Cut the moon and clouds from the monochrome design and use them as a mask on the spatter-painted background.*

CHAPTER 19

Spatter-Painted Paper-Cuts

THE SPATTERED-PAINT TECHNIQUE need not be limited to use in the backgrounds of paper-cuts; it can create some striking effects on the surface of the cuts themselves as well. Spatter-painting paper-cuts involves masking techniques similar to those used in painting backgrounds. Again, because of the many variations possible, we shall cover only the basic procedures, upon which innovations can be built.

The materials are the same here as for the previous spatter-painted projects. I strongly recommend tempera paints, especially when applying color to black paper, because they are richer and brighter in color than regular watercolors.

PROCEDURE 1

As with spatter-painted backgrounds, the easiest type of spatter-painted paper-cut to make is that requiring only one color.

1. Make your monochrome cut.
2. Choose an appropriate background paper.
3. Mount the monochrome cut on the background.
4. Spatter paint on the mounted cut (Figure 1).

FIGURE 1

PROCEDURE 2

When you want several colors in the cut, apply paint to the paper *before* cutting out the design. It is, of course, possible to apply the paint after the cut has been made, but that way the paper is more difficult to handle. I suggest that at least in the beginning you follow this method.

1. Carefully make a sketch for your cut.
2. Prepare your background paper as you did in Chapter 17 (Figure 1, opposite page).
3. Using your sketch as a guide, cut out masks to cover the various areas of the paper you will be using for your cut where you do *not* want paint.
4. Using your first mask, apply the first color to the paper you will use for your cut (Figure 2). Allow the paint to dry.
5. Using your second mask, apply the second color (Figure 3). Allow the paint to dry.
6. Repeat this procedure for each color you apply.
7. When all the colors have been applied, your paper is ready for cutting (Figure 4).
8. Tape your sketch carefully to the prepared paper, and complete your cut as you have done in previous projects.
9. Mount your completed cut on the background you prepared in step 2 (Figure 5).

FIGURE 1

FIGURE 2

FIGURE 3

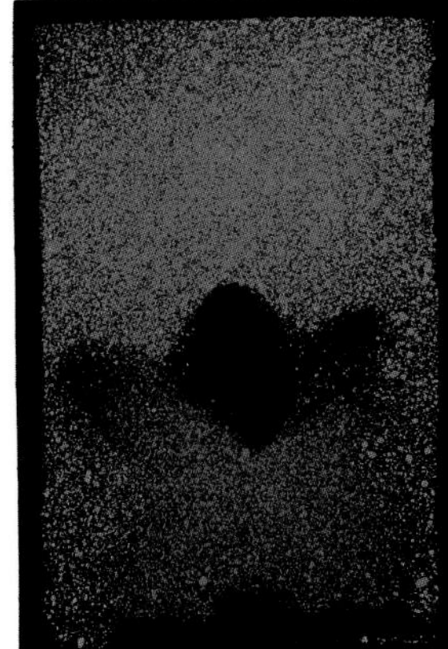
FIGURE 4

FIGURE 5

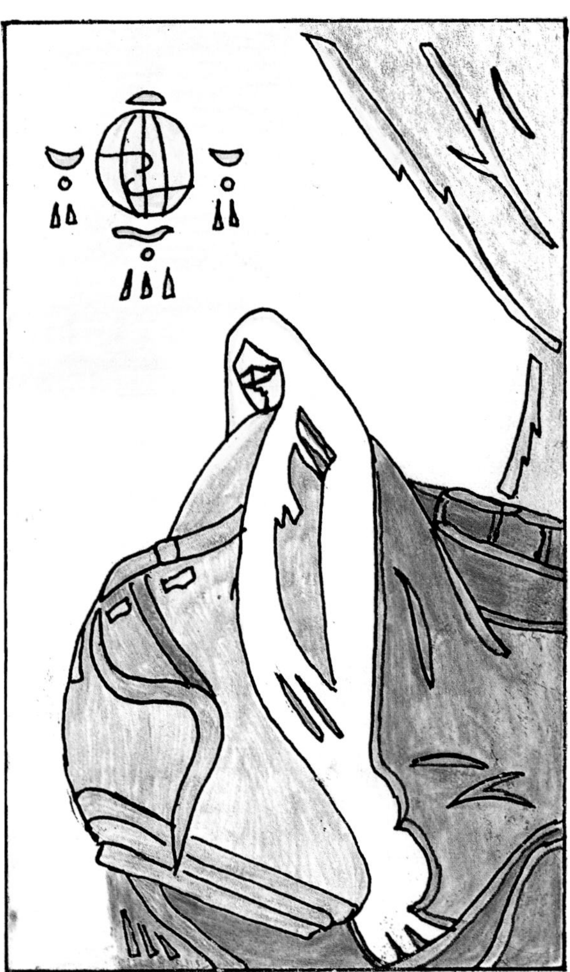

FIGURE 1

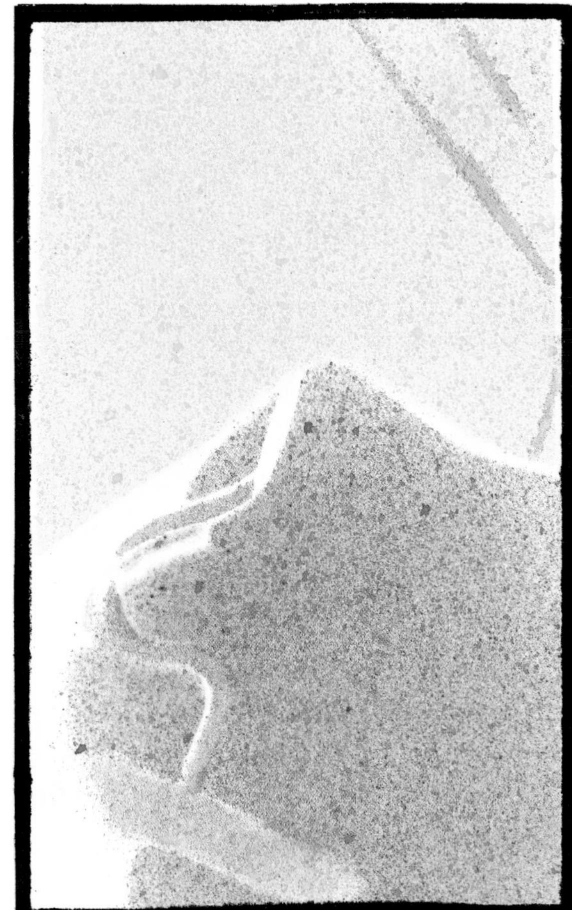

FIGURE 2

You can achieve interesting effects with a double cut—that is, mounting one cut, such as a fence, a grove of trees, or a window frame, on top of another.

1. Make a careful sketch of your design so you can use it as a pattern not only for your cut but also for the masks necessary when you apply spattered paint (Figure 1).
2. Prepare your background paper as you did in Chapter 17 (Figure 2).
3. Begin preparing the paper from which you will make your first cut by cutting out the mask for the first application of spattered paint. Apply the paint (Figure 3) and let it dry.
4. Repeat this procedure for the second color (Figure 4), and once again for the third color (Figure 5). Follow these same instructions for the application of any additional colors.
5. Your paper should now be ready for cutting.
6. Make your first cut just as you did earlier monochrome cuts, and mount it to the background you prepared in step 2 (Figure 6).
7. Decide on the design for the second cut. (In this example, I have used the pattern of a grille found in ancient Japanese homes.)
8. Prepare the paper for your second cut.
9. Cut out the second design (Figure 7).
10. Carefully glue the second cut over the first (Figure 8, over).

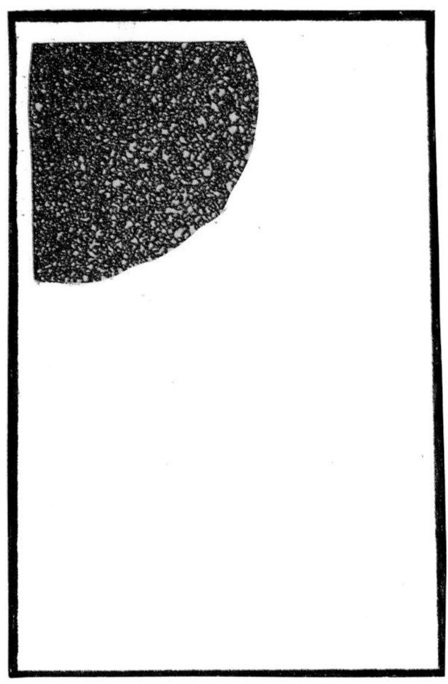

FIGURE 3

FIGURE 4

FIGURE 5

FIGURE 6

FIGURE 7

FIGURE 8

PROCEDURE 4

The technique involved here is a bit complicated, requiring that the entire picture be cut into individual sections; each section is spatter-painted separately, and then the picture is put back together, almost as if it were a jigsaw puzzle. The technique is most effective for creating landscapes and seascapes where various shadings of color are needed to give a feeling of depth.

It is a good idea, at least in the beginning, to create designs that use large blocks of paper, since a few large pieces are much easier to handle than numerous small ones. One general rule to remember in setting up designs for this kind of cut is that distant objects are lighter in color than those in the foreground; therefore, be sure to choose a color for the foreground of your cut that is dark enough to allow for shading to a lighter background.

1. Draw your design (Figure 1), dividing it into specific sections according to the perspective you wish to achieve.

2. Choose the color for your cut. Although I have used blue in the example shown here, the picture could also be done in green, purple, brown, orange—any color that will allow for shading. You could also use a combination of colors; however, for the first practice design it would be better to stay with a single hue.

3. Tape your design to the colored paper. Cut out the small details first, such as the three scholars in this example. Then cut the picture into its several sections (Figure 2).

4. Prepare your background paper as you did in the previous spatter-painted projects (Figure 3, over).

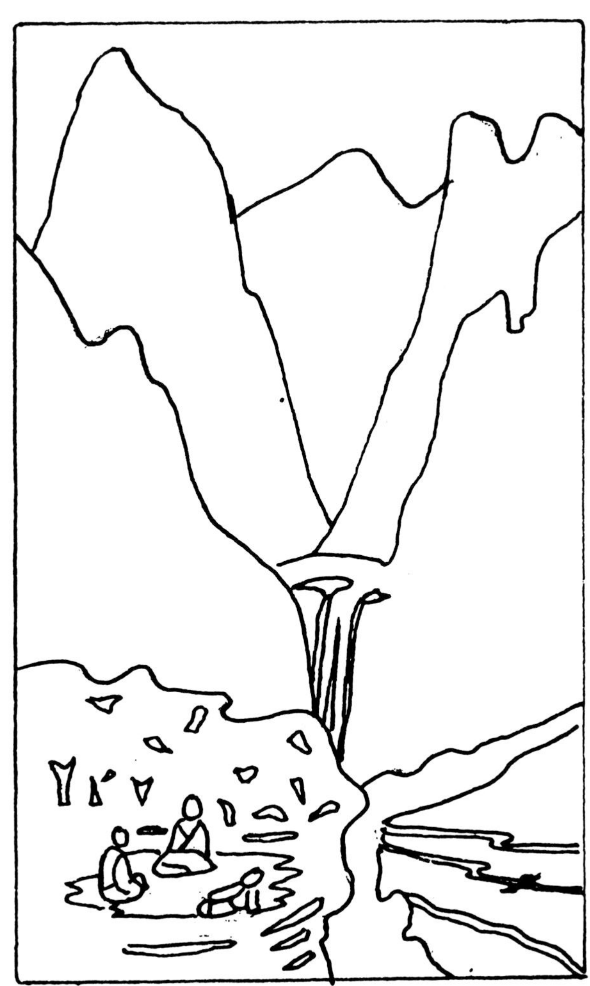

FIGURE 1

FIGURE 2

5. You are now ready to paint the individual sections of your cut and apply them to the background. Follow a numbered sequence like the one shown here (Figure 4).

6. Section 1 is the closest to the foreground, so it should be painted the darkest color; in this example it is spatter-painted black. Allow the cut to dry, then glue it in place on your prepared background (Figure 5).

7. Section 2 is painted a slightly lighter color. Allow the cut to dry, then carefully glue it in place (Figure 6).

8. Sections 3 and 4 are spatter-painted a darker color on their inner edges only. Allow them to dry, then carefully glue each into place in numerical order (Figure 7).

9. Sections 5 and 6 are spatter-painted a darker color on their inner edges, with the remainder spatter-painted white. After they have dried, mount section 5 first, then section 6 (Figure 8).

10. Section 7, the most distant element in the landscape, should be the lightest color, so it gets a heavy coat of white paint only. Let it dry, and then glue it into place (Figure 9).

11. Your picture is now complete (Figure 10, page 128).

Note: If you were to add another range of mountains in the distance, you would need to change to a lighter colored paper and spatter-paint it white. Beyond that, change to white paper and spatter-paint it with a color lighter than that of the body of your cut.

FIGURE 3

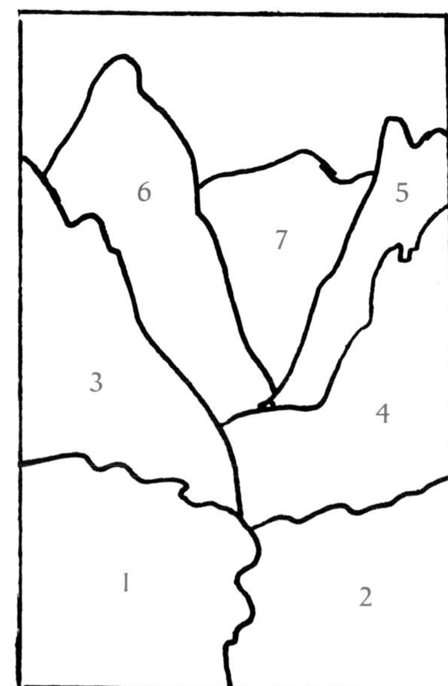

FIGURE 4

FIGURE 5

FIGURE 6

FIGURE 7

FIGURE 8

FIGURE 9

FIGURE 10

PRACTICE DESIGN

PRACTICE DESIGN *for a two-cut picture. The design on the facing page is meant to be placed over the carp, an image adapted from a wood-block print by Hokusai (1760–1849).*

CHAPTER 20

THE LANTERN DANCE, *after an illustration by Katharine Sturges.*

Framing and Displaying Cut-Art

LIKE THE OLD ADAGE about children, cut-art is meant to be seen, and after spending many long hours creating your pictures you will certainly want to display them to their best advantage. Because these works are fragile, you will also want to give them some protection so that they can continue to give you pleasure through the years.

Displaying Cut-Art in the Japanese Style

Paintings and other works of art are rarely displayed permanently in the traditional Japanese home. Rather, one or two main pieces are changed according to season or mood. On special occasions, such as when an important guest is invited to the home, a work of art appropriate to the guest's interests and status is displayed. To make these changes quickly and easily, the Japanese have developed a simple method that works quite well with paper-cuts and adapts beautifully to the Western home, often with very contemporary and sophisticated results.

For works of art to be interchanged with the least amount of trouble, they must be fairly standard in both size and shape. The Japanese have accomplished this with the *tanzaku* and the *shikishi*, described on pages 138–144.

Paper Plate Mount

A simple and inexpensive way to display your finished cuts is to mount them on plain paper plates. Hung in groups, they make a delightful and decorative addition to a child's room or family room.

MATERIALS

Completed paper-cuts, mounted or unmounted, small enough to fit the center of a paper plate

Paper plates (preferably the white, plastic-coated kind, which can be wiped clean of dust with a soft cloth)

Water-soluble white glue or adhesive spray

String or ribbon

Scissors

Self-adhesive vinyl or Mylar (optional)

PROCEDURE

1. Using white glue or spray adhesive, carefully mount the paper-cut in the center of the plate (Figure 1).
2. Make two small holes at the top of the plate. Insert string or ribbon, and tie a loop for hanging.
3. If you wish to apply a protective covering, cut a circle of self-adhesive vinyl or Mylar slightly larger than your picture and, following the manufacturer's instructions, place it over the image.

FIGURE 1

Plastic Mount

One of the easiest and least expensive ways to show off unmounted monochrome cuts is to arrange them in a window much the way the Chinese once displayed their "window flowers." Although some collectors actually do paste their cuts directly to the window glass, I do not recommend this, since the only way to remove them is with a razor blade. Who wants to see hours of work destroyed in that manner? Instead, I suggest that you encase unmounted monochrome cuts in clear plastic, then display them in the window. Department stores, office supply stores, and arts and crafts shops carry various types of self-adhesive vinyl or Mylar such as Con-Tact, Magic Cover, and 20th-Century Seal Plastic Film, any of which can be used for permanently laminating your cuts in plastic. Simply follow the manufacturer's instructions.

MATERIALS

Completed monochrome paper-cut

Acetate folders

Clear or colored plastic tape (the color should match that of your cut)

Water-soluble white glue

Scissors

Ruler

FIGURE 1

PROCEDURE

1. Cut the acetate folder to a size that will accommodate your cut. Make the folder at least ¾–1″ (1.9–2.5 cm) larger than the picture if you are using colored plastic tape to bind it, since the tape also acts as a frame; you don't want your picture to look crowded. If you are using clear plastic tape, cut the folder at least ½″ (1.3 cm) larger than your picture.

2. Using a few drops of white glue on the back of your cut, center the picture *inside* the trimmed folder (Figure 1).

3. Carefully bind the four edges of the cover with clear or colored plastic tape (Figure 2). Follow this same procedure for cuts laminated in self-sealing plastic sheets.

4. The sealed cut can now be attached to a window with clear tape.

FIGURE 2

Framing Paper-Cuts

In the West the most popular way to display finished paper-cuts is to frame them and hang them on a wall. The frame not only protects the picture but also provides a natural transition between the picture and the wall on which it hangs.

I personally prefer to have my most valuable works framed by a professional. This can become a bit expensive, however, so you may wish to try your own hand at framing, at least in the beginning.

Choosing a Frame

Choosing an appropriate frame is most often a matter of individual taste; nonetheless, there are several important points you should consider.

Because monochrome paper-cuts have a light and delicate appearance, you must take care to pick a frame that does not overwhelm the picture. Avoid brightly colored or ornate frames; the best choices are simple wooden or metal frames in black, brown, gold, or silver (Example 1). Bamboo frames are also very effective. Painted and appliquéd paper-cuts can hold their own in more ornate frames (Example 2) if the design of the frame is not too busy.

EXAMPLE 1

EXAMPLE 2

EXAMPLE 3

EXAMPLE 4

Unlike oil paintings, paper-cuts do not have a protective coating, and should thus be framed under glass to guard against dust, dirt, and smoke. Be sure to choose a frame that is large enough to accommodate both a mat and the picture without looking cramped.

Choosing a Mat

Matting your picture is important for both esthetic and practical reasons. The mat not only provides a transition between the picture and the frame but also keeps the picture from sticking to the glass, creating a dead-air space that allows for changes in humidity and temperature. Because making your own mats can be a tedious job, with often unsatisfactory results, I recommend that you buy commercially made mats, which are available at art supply shops or arts and crafts stores. As with frames, there are several points to consider in choosing an appropriate mat.

Light, neutral tones—tan, beige, cream, or gray—or light pastel colors are usually most satisfactory (Example 3). For a painted or appliquéd paper-cut, choose a mat similar in hue to one of the colors in your picture (Example 4). An acid-free board such as museum board is the best material. Over time, inexpensive mats made of wood pulp containing acid will permanently discolor your picture.

For esthetic reasons, choose a mat that is wider at the bottom than at the top and sides. For example, a mat 2″ (5.1 cm) wide on the top and sides should be 2½″ (6.4 cm) on the bottom. This will keep your picture from looking as if it might fall from the frame when it is hung.

MATERIALS

Mounted paper-cut

Picture frame with glass

Mat, preferably acid-free, cut so the opening covers ¼″ (0.64 cm) of each side of your picture surface

Mounting board made of acid-free, 4-ply cardboard, cut to same size as outside dimensions of mat

Corrugated cardboard, cut to same size as mounting board

Gummed paper hinges (the kind used to mount stamps in an album)

Brads or small nails

Pliers

Brown wrapping paper

Water-soluble white glue

2 screw eyes and wire for hanging

Ruler

Scissors

X-Acto knife

Pencil

PROCEDURE

1. Make a folder of the mat and the mounting board by joining them at the top with several gummed paper hinges (Figure 1).
2. Place the picture on the mounting board and fold the mat down to make certain that the picture is properly positioned. Adjust if necessary.
3. Fold the mat up once more. Hold the picture in place and

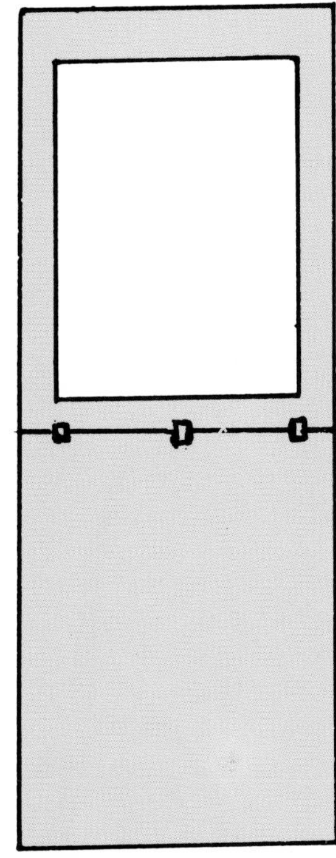

FIGURE 1

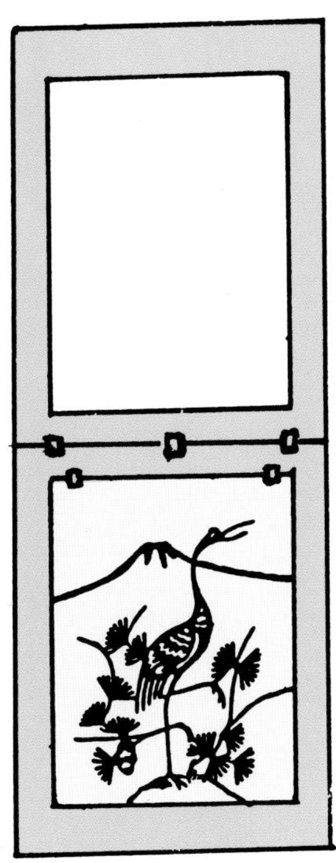

FIGURE 2

carefully attach it to the mounting board with gummed hinges at the two upper corners only (Figure 2). Do not use masking or transparent tape.
4. Fold the mat down over the picture once more. Make certain that the picture has not slipped, and readjust if necessary.
5. Clean the glass of your frame, making certain that it is free of smudges and moisture.
6. Place the glass in the frame, and turn both face down on a clean work surface.
7. Place the matted picture in the frame.
8. Place the corrugated cardboard on top of the matted picture.
9. Using the *side* of the pliers, carefully push brads or small nails into the inside edge of the frame parallel to the mat and backing at intervals of 1½–2″ (3.8–5.1 cm).
10. Cut a piece of brown wrapping paper slightly larger than your frame.
11. Dampen the paper slightly with a sponge. (The paper will become tight as it dries.)
12. Apply water-soluble white glue to the back of the *frame* (not on the corrugated backing).
13. Stretch the damp paper over the back of the frame, and press it down firmly onto the glue. Allow the paper to dry.
14. Using an X-Acto knife and a ruler, trim the excess paper by cutting it ⅛″ (0.32 cm) inside the outer edge of the frame.
15. Attach screw eyes and wire to the frame for hanging.
16. As with all works of fine art, hang your picture out of direct sunlight. This will help keep it from fading so it can give you years of enjoyment.

Traditional Tanzaku and Tanzakukake

The *tanzaku* is a long, narrow piece of cardboard similar in weight to 4-ply poster board. It comes in one standard size—2⅜ × 14¼″ (6.1 × 36.2 cm)—and is available in a variety of light colors such as white, cream, tan, gold, and pastel pink. *Tanzaku* are usually available at Japanese specialty and art shops; you can, however, make a substitute that works very well with *kiri-e* by simply cutting 4-ply poster board to the standard *tanzaku* size. Naturally, paper-cuts mounted on *tanzaku* have to be long and narrow, as in the example at right.

The traditional method for displaying the finished *tanzaku* is to fasten it to a *tanzakukake*, a long, slender piece of wood suspended by a cord from a nail or picture hanger. Both the traditional *tanzakukake* and a modern alternative are very simple to make.

MATERIALS

Piece of wood (preferably with an interesting grain) measuring 3⅜″ wide × 25⅜″ long × ¼–⅜″ thick (8.6 × 64.5 cm × 0.64–0.95 cm)

Black cord (macramé cord works well)

Drill with a small bit about ⅛″ (0.32 cm) in diameter

Wood saw

Keyhole saw or jigsaw (optional)

Fine-grain sandpaper

Ruler

Scissors

Pencil

PROCEDURE

1. Carefully saw your long piece of wood into one of the traditional shapes shown here (Figure 1, opposite).
2. Drill a hole for the hanging cord 1¾″ (4.5 cm) from the top of your board, making certain it is centered.
3. If you use *tanzakukake* design 1 or 2, cut the cloud shape at the bottom of the board with a keyhole saw or jigsaw (optional).
4. Choose one of the following methods for attaching the cords that will hold the *tanzaku* to the *tanzakukake*, and proceed according to the instructions.

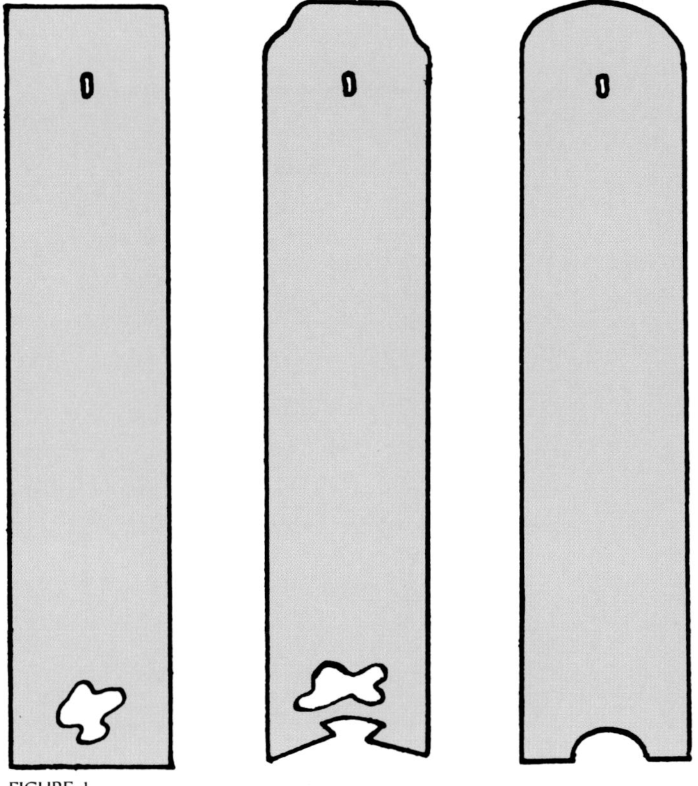
FIGURE 1

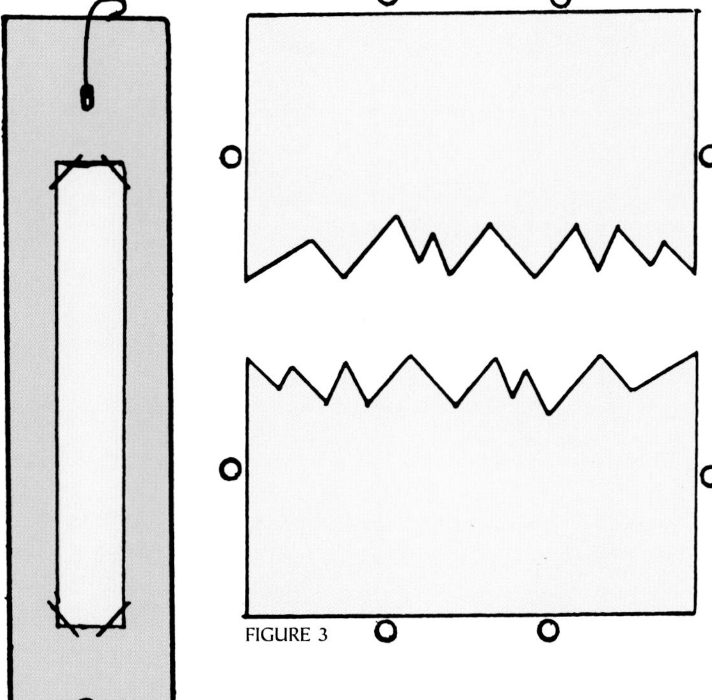
FIGURE 2

FIGURE 3

Cord Attachment Method One

With this method, the *tanzaku* is held in place by pieces of black cord tied across each of its corners (Figure 2).

1. Measure down 4¾″ (12.1 cm) from the top of your board. Draw a line as a top register mark for the *tanzaku*.
2. Place the *tanzaku* on the board, and draw a line as a bottom register mark.
3. Using your ruler to center the *tanzaku,* draw lines down each of its sides. You now have a complete outline of the *tanzaku* on your board.
4. Along the top of the *tanzaku* outline, measure in ¾″ (1.9 cm) from each side with your ruler and mark the two spots just above the top line. These will be your drill guides. The holes must be *outside* the outline so your *tanzaku* will fit.
5. Measure down ¾″ (1.9 cm) from the top of the *tanzaku* outline on each side. Make your drill marks.
6. Repeat this procedure at the bottom of the outline. You should now have eight drill marks on your board.
7. Carefully drill a hole through each of the marks (Figure 3).
8. Sand your board until all rough edges are quite smooth and all pencil marks are removed. Do not paint the board; leave it in its natural condition.
9. Cut four pieces of black cord, each 6″ (15.2 cm) long. Thread one piece across each of the corners and tie the ends in back. Cut off any excess.
10. Thread another piece of cord through the hole at the top of your board and tie the ends together.
11. Slip your *tanzaku* into place, and hang for display.

Cord Attachment Method Two

This method differs from the first only in the placement of the cord.

1. Follow the first three steps of method 1 above.
2. Make a drill mark at each top corner of the *tanzaku* outline.
3. Measure down ⅝″ (1.6 cm) from the top on each side and make two more drill marks.
4. Measure up ½″ (1.3 cm) on each side from the bottom and make drill marks.
5. Measure in ⅞″ (2.2 cm) from each side on the bottom and make drill marks.
6. Carefully drill a hole through each of your drill marks.
7. Sand your board.
8. Cut two pieces of black cord, each 10″ (25.4 cm) long. At the top of the board, thread the cord through the holes to form an X (Figure 4). Tie the ends of the cord in back and trim any excess.
9. At the bottom of the board, thread the cord through the holes to form an asymmetrical X (Figure 5). Tie the ends of the cord in back.
10. Cut a piece of hanging cord, thread it through the top hole, and tie the ends together. Slip your *tanzaku* in place and display (Figure 6).

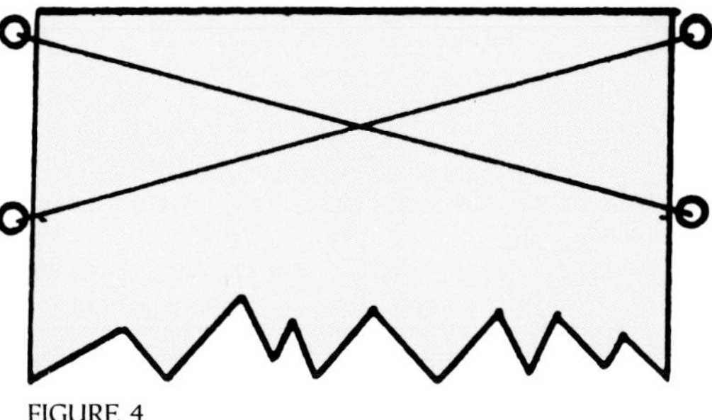

FIGURE 4

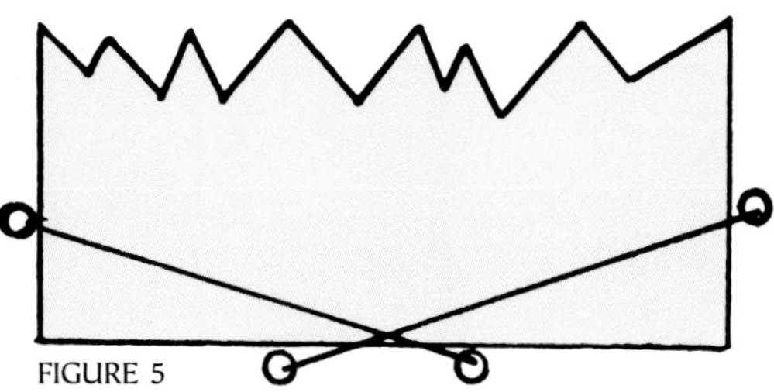

FIGURE 5

FIGURE 6

Alternative Tanzakukake

A simple alternative to the traditional *tanzakukake* can be made with heavy cardboard covered with paper. If you use gift wrap as a covering, choose one that is fairly heavy and has a small and subdued design. Stay with light colors such as tan, pastel blue, pastel green, or gray.

MATERIALS

Piece of heavy cardboard measuring 25⅜ × 3⅜″ (64.5 × 8.6 cm)

Self-adhesive plastic (such as Con-Tact) in a wood-grain pattern, or brown wrapping paper or gift wrap

Black cord

Water-soluble white glue

Ruler

Scissors

Pencil

FIGURE 1

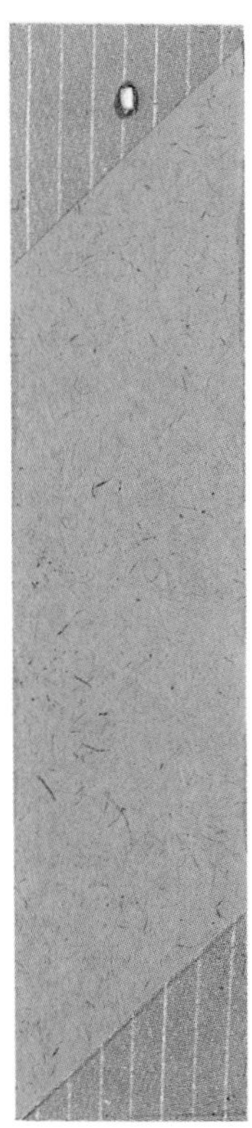

FIGURE 2

PROCEDURE

1. Cut your cardboard to the correct size, making sure that you have no rough, jagged edges.
2. If you choose to cover your *tanzakukake* with self-adhesive plastic (Figure 1), follow the manufacturer's directions.
3. If you instead use brown wrapping paper or gift wrap, attach the paper to the cardboard with white glue (Figure 2).
4. Follow steps 1–3 of cord attachment method 1 above to make your *tanzaku* outline. If you are using brown paper or gift wrap, make your outline quite light so that it can be erased later.
5. Decide which cord attachment method you wish to use and mark your cord holes according to that procedure.
6. With small scissors or another sharp-pointed instrument, carefully punch holes for all the cords, including the hole for the hanging cord at the top.
7. Gently erase all pencil marks.
8. Cut your cord according to the method of attachment you are using, thread it through the holes, and tie the ends together.
9. Slip your *tanzaku* into place and hang it for display.

Traditional Shikishi and Shikifuku

Shikishi are rectangular pieces of cardboard similar in weight to 10-ply poster board, with narrow (1/8"/0.32 cm) gold-foil trim (Figure 1). They come in two standard sizes—9½ × 10¼" (24.1 × 26.0 cm) and 10¼ × 19" (26.0 × 48.3 cm)—and are also available in a variety of light colors such as white, gold, silver, and pastel brown, green, yellow, cream, or pink. Like *tanzaku*, they are usually available at Japanese specialty and art shops; an adequate substitute can be made by cutting 10-ply poster board to either of the two standard sizes. The narrow gold trim can be made from gold gift wrap; however, you may find that your picture is just as effective without it.

The traditional method for displaying the *shikishi* is to attach it, by means of elastic cord across each corner, to a *shikifuku*, a scroll of paper-backed brocaded silk suspended by a cord from a nail or picture hanger. Like the *tanzakukake*, the *shikifuku* allows you to change pictures often and easily so that, as one Asian art connoisseur has said, "you will see all your [works] and they will never suffer damage by drafts or sun rays. Moreover, . . . you will never tire of them."

The procedure described here for creating a traditional *shikifuku* is for the smaller of the two standard *shikishi* sizes.

FIGURE 1

MATERIALS

Silk brocade, 23 × 12″ (58.4 × 30.5 cm), in a light color with a small, subdued pattern

Brown wrapping paper cut to same size as silk brocade

Wax paper

Elastic thread

Needle with eye large enough for the elastic thread

Flat silk cord or ribbon, 7½ × ¼″ (19.1 × 0.6 cm)

2 pieces of 10-ply poster board, each 10¾ × ¾″ (27.3 × 1.9 cm)

Adhesive spray

X-Acto knife

Ruler

Scissors

Pencil

PROCEDURE

1. Cover a large, clean working surface with wax paper and spread your wrapping paper out on it.

2. Following the manufacturer's instructions, apply a thin coating of spray adhesive along the top edge of the wrapping paper. Do not apply too much; it should not soak through the silk you put over it in the next step. You may want to practice with a few scraps first.

3. Align the top of your silk with the top of the brown paper, making certain that the two layers will fit neatly together down their full length.

4. Press the top of the silk firmly to the paper and smooth out any wrinkles.

5. Working down the length of the paper about 6″ (15 cm) at a time, spray on the adhesive and press the silk into place, making certain each time that there are no wrinkles. Allow the silk and paper to dry.

6. Put down a clean surface of wax paper and turn your *shikifuku* over, silk face down. From this point on, make all pencil markings on the paper *back* of the *shikifuku*.

7. Measure down 1½″ (3.81 cm) from the top of the *shikifuku* and draw a line across the paper.

8. Center one of the 10¾ × ¾″ (27.3 × 1.9 cm) strips of poster board along the line you have just drawn, and glue it in place (Figure 2).

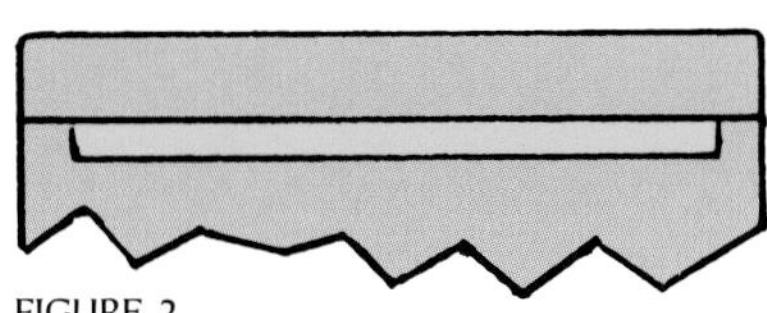

FIGURE 2

9. Carefully apply adhesive to the 1½″ (3.81 cm) strip of silk above the cardboard; fold the silk firmly down over the cardboard and hold in place until it is secure. Smooth out any wrinkles.

10. Measure up 1½″ (3.81 cm) from the bottom of the *shikifuku*; draw your line, and repeat steps 8 and 9. Your *shikifuku* should now measure 20″ (50.8 cm) long.

11. Measure down 4½″ (11.4 cm) from the top of the *shikifuku* and draw a line across the paper.

12. Place the top of the *shikishi* (the narrow side) along this line. Using your ruler, center the *shikishi* along the line and outline it in pencil as you did for the *tanzaku*.

13. Measure in 1″ (2.5 cm) from the top left-hand corner of the *shikishi* outline and make a mark. Then measure down 1″ (2.5 cm) from the top along the left side, and make another mark (Figure 3).

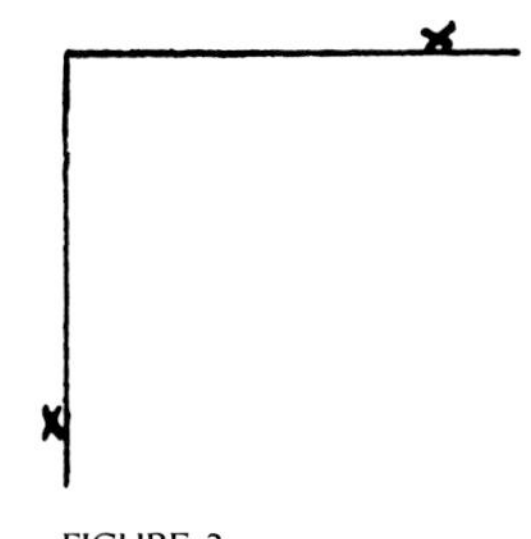

FIGURE 3

14. Repeat this at each of the four corners so that you have eight marks—two at each corner (Figure 4).

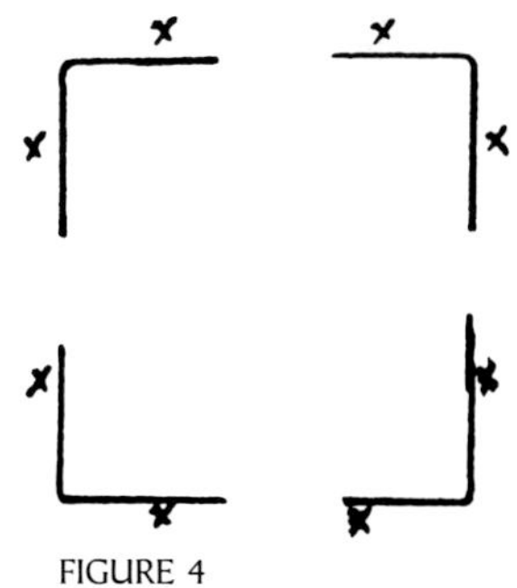

FIGURE 4

15. Thread your needle with a length of the elastic thread and, from the back side, carefully push the needle and thread through one of your corner marks. Bring the thread across the front of the *shikifuku* and down into the mark diagonally opposite the point where you started (Figure 5). Tie the thread in back, being careful not to stretch it tight. You have now completed one mounting corner.

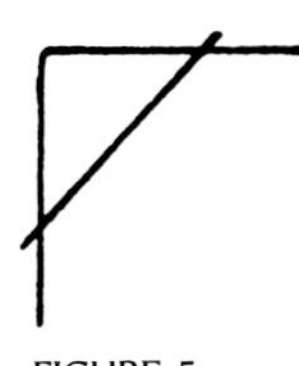

FIGURE 5

16. Repeat step 15 for each of the other three corners. Your *shikishi* should now slip very easily into the four mounting corners (Figure 6).

FIGURE 6

17. Using your ruler, measure to the center of the top of the *shikifuku*; then measure down ¾″ (1.91 cm) and make a mark, which should be just below the edge of the card-board reinforcement (Figure 7).

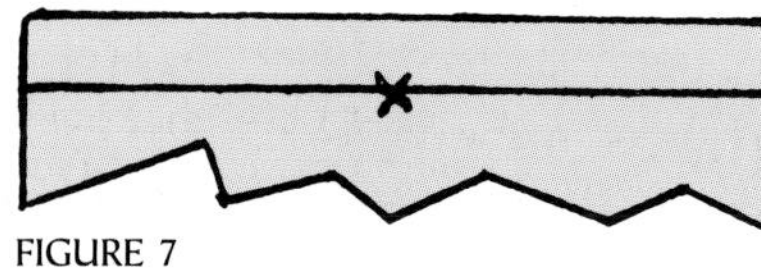

FIGURE 7

18. With your X-Acto knife, carefully cut a ¼″ (0.6 cm) slit on the mark you just drew.
19. Fold your length of flat cord or ribbon in half; measure down about 1¾″ (4.5 cm) and tie a square knot so that you have a loop and two long ends (Figure 8).

FIGURE 8

20. From the front of the *shikifuku*, carefully push the *loop* of the tied cord or ribbon through the slit you made in step 18. The knot and two long ends of the cord stay on the front side (Figure 9).

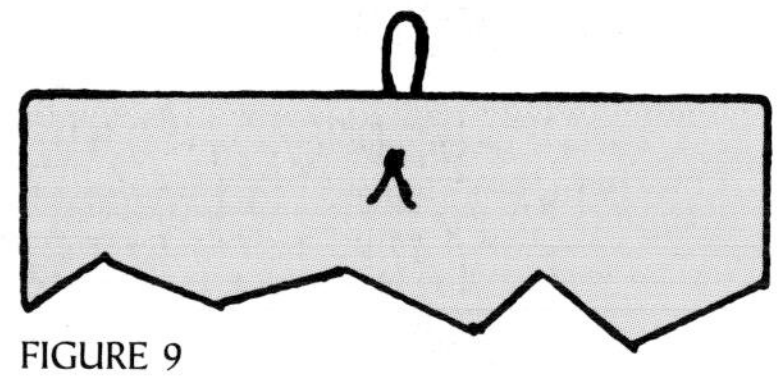

FIGURE 9

21. Hang your *shikifuku* by the looped cord for display (Figure 10).

FIGURE 10

Mat-Mounted Shikishi

MATERIALS

Matchstick bamboo place mat at least 12 × 19″ (30.5 × 48.3 cm)

Cord or heavy string for making corner mounts

Needle with eye large enough for the cord or string

Silk tassel (optional); usually available at electrical supply stores as decorative light pulls

Scissors

Ruler

Felt-tip pen

PROCEDURE

1. Place the mat on your working surface. Place the *shikishi* vertically on the mat 4″ (10.2 cm) down from the top.
2. With your ruler, measure to make certain that the *shikishi* is centered from left to right.
3. Mark the corners of the *shikishi* lightly on the mat with the felt-tip pen. (Consider this the *back* of your picture mounting.)
4. To make the cord mounts for each of the four corners of the *shikishi*, follow steps 13–15 of the traditional *shikifuku* instructions above.
5. Tie the cord for hanging at the top of the mat, as in the illustration at the top of page 145.
6. If you are using the decorative tassel, tie it in place at the bottom of the mat.
7. Mount your *shikishi* in place and hang for display. Easy, wasn't it?

Tray-Mounted Shikishi

Mat-mounted shikishi.

MATERIALS

Flat bamboo or wicker tray at least 17″ (43.2 cm) in diameter

Elastic thread or cord

Needle with eye large enough for elastic thread or cord

Cord for hanging

Scissors

PROCEDURE

1. Center your *shikishi* in the tray.
2. Using the needle and elastic thread or cord, make four corner mounts for the *shikishi*. (See step 15 of the instructions for the traditional *shikifuku*.)
3. Tie a cord for hanging at the top of the tray as shown in the illustration below. Mount your *shikishi* and hang it for display.

Tray-mounted shikishi.

CHAPTER 21

Other Uses for Cut-Art

As you read in the history of cut-art, the Chinese and Japanese use paper-cuts for many decorative purposes besides hanging framed works for display. You can do the same. In this chapter, I suggest several possibilities; your own imagination and creativity should certainly lead to countless others.

Materials for most of these projects should be readily available; for any that may be difficult to locate, consult the list of mail-order suppliers at the back of this book. The projects are well worth the extra time and effort.

Japanese flat fan (uchiwa). *Actual size.*

Candleholder

MATERIALS

Clear, straight-sided drinking glass at least 4½″ (11.4 cm) high and 9″ (22.9 cm) in circumference

Completed monochrome paper-cut in a size suitable for the glass

Clear glass votive candleholder small enough to fit inside the drinking glass

Votive candle

Spray fixative

Spray adhesive

Design for a candleholder.

PROCEDURE

1. Wash and dry the glass, making certain that you remove all grease, smudges, or other residue.
2. Spray the front of the paper-cut with fixative; this protective coating will allow you to wipe the cut clean with a damp cloth whenever dust accumulates on the candleholder.
3. Spray the back of the paper-cut with adhesive, and carefully mount the paper-cut on the side of the glass. The easiest way to do this is to place the glass on its side.
4. Make certain that all parts of the cut are glued securely to the glass. Allow it to dry.
5. If the glass has become smudged, wipe it carefully with a damp cloth. *Never submerge or soak your candleholder.*
6. Place the votive candle and holder inside your glass. Light the candle; relax, and enjoy.

Design for a lampshade.

Lampshade

MATERIALS

Straight-sided lampshade made of paper, plastic, or parchment

Completed monochrome paper-cut (see design on page 148)

Spray fixative

Spray adhesive

Lint-free cloth

PROCEDURE

1. With the lint-free cloth, wipe all dust from the lampshade.
2. Spray the front of the paper-cut with fixative. This provides a protective coating so you can wipe the cut with a damp cloth whenever the shade needs cleaning. *Never submerge or soak the lampshade.*
3. Place the lampshade on its side. Spray the back of the paper-cut with adhesive, and carefully center the paper-cut on the side of the shade.
4. Make certain that all parts of the cut are securely glued to the shade. Allow it to dry.
5. Place the finished shade on your lamp.

Japanese Flat Fan (Uchiwa)

The Japanese flat fan (*uchiwa*) has traditionally been a thing of both beauty and practicality. Originally used to fan the kitchen fire, today the *uchiwa* is used to cool oneself on warm summer days. The beautiful pictures usually printed on these fans are intended to give pleasure to the mind as well as to the body. Hung on the wall, the flat fan also makes a delightful decorative display.

Oriental specialty and gift shops sometimes have flat, bamboo-handle fans made of plain white paper, an excellent mounting surface for paper-cuts. More common is the kind made of cardboard with a picture printed on it. These cardboard fans can still be used for mounting paper-cuts, however; to prepare the surface, simply cover the handle with masking tape and spray the fan with several coats of paint until the print is no longer visible. Let the fan dry and remove the tape from the handle.

MATERIALS

Japanese flat fan

Finished paper-cut to mount on fan (see page 146 and design below)

Spray fixative

Spray adhesive

PROCEDURE

1. Give your paper-cut a protective coating of spray fixative.
2. Place your fan on a clean work surface.
3. Spray the back of your paper-cut with adhesive, and carefully mount it in place on the fan.
4. Press down gently on the paper-cut to make certain that all edges are securely glued to the fan. Allow it to dry.

Design for an uchiwa *(Japanese flat fan).*

Découpaged Boxes and Plaques

Paper-cuts, particularly those made of thinner paper such as origami paper, lend themselves beautifully to découpage. The technique described here for decorating boxes or plaques works equally well for other projects where wood serves as the mounting base. Découpage finish is preferable to clear varnish, which takes longer to dry and tends to yellow with age.

Design for a box or plaque.

Découpaged plaque.

MATERIALS

Completed paper-cut of a size suitable for your box or plaque

Plain wooden box or plaque (available in several sizes and shapes at most craft or hobby shops)

Water-soluble white glue

Enamel paint (optional)

Découpage finish (or clear varnish)

Spray fixative

Brush cleaner such as turpentine; use what the manufacturer of your finish recommends

Small sable brush

#600 wet/dry sandpaper

#0000 steel wool

Vinegar

Cotton swabs

Lint-free cloth

Paste wax

PROCEDURE

1. Sand the surface of your box or plaque until it is free of all nicks and scratches. Finish smoothing with a piece of steel wool.
2. Clean the wood surface with a lint-free cloth to remove all residue from the steel wool and sandpaper.
3. If you are painting your plaque or box, follow the paint manufacturer's directions. If more than one coat of paint is needed, sand the surface lightly between applications and wipe with the lint-free cloth.
4. Apply a coat of spray fixative to your paper-cut. This will help to prevent the color from running when the finish coat is applied.
5. Apply water-soluble white glue to the back of your paper-cut and mount it on the box or plaque, making certain that all edges are firmly glued to the wood. Remove any excess glue from around the edges with a cotton swab dipped in vinegar. Allow to dry.
6. Using a sable brush, apply the first coat of finish according to the manufacturer's directions. Brush in one direction only, and carefully remove any hairs that may come loose from your brush.
7. Allow the finish coat to dry. Time will vary according to the type of finish you are using. Avoid putting down a second coat before the first one is dry, or your finish will streak or ripple.
8. Continue to apply the finish, allowing it to dry between each application, until the surface is smooth and you can no longer feel the paper-cut with your fingers.
9. Once your final coat is dry, carefully sand the surface with *wet* sandpaper. Allow it to dry, then wipe it clean with the lint-free cloth.
10. Rub the finished surface with steel wool using a circular movement until the finish is glassy smooth. Wipe clean.
11. Rub the entire finished surface with paste wax until it shines.

Mugs

A new and intriguing line of plastic ware on which you can mount artwork is now on the market (see the source list at the back of this book) and should pique the creative interests of artists, craftsmen, and hobbyists alike. Bowls, plates, tumblers, steins, and mugs are available; each unit consists of an inner plastic liner, a clear outer liner, and a paper pattern on which art can be mounted and placed between the inner and outer liners. Using your paper-cuts in such a manner lets you design highly attractive and unusual gifts (I've made several dozen already).

The instructions given here for the mug work for the other items as well.

MATERIALS

Two-piece plastic mug with paper pattern insert

Completed paper-cut (see design below)

Spray adhesive or rubber cement for mounting

Clear self-adhesive plastic or Mylar

Scissors

PROCEDURE

1. Using spray adhesive or rubber cement, mount your completed paper-cut on the paper pattern supplied with the mug. (If you prefer a colored background, trace the paper pattern onto colored paper, cut it out, and mount your paper-cut on that surface first.)

2. Cut two sheets of clear self-adhesive plastic or Mylar slightly larger than your mounted cut. Following the manufacturer's directions, laminate your mounted paper-cut between the two sheets and trim off the excess. I recommend laminating your cuts to protect them from possible water damage during washing, as the seal on the plastic ware is not completely water-tight.

3. Separate the two sections of the mug by twisting and pulling them apart.

4. Place your picture in the clear outside section of the mug. Replace the inner lining, and push the two parts firmly together.

5. Although the manufacturer warns against placing this plastic ware in a dishwasher, cleaning your mug is easy: Simply take it apart and remove the artwork first, then wash, dry, and reassemble. Nothing to it!

Miniature Folding Screens

Paper-cuts mounted on miniature Japanese folding screens can create a charming background for a small figurine or a tiny bouquet of flowers. Plain gold screens are available in three standard sizes: 7¼ × 10½″ (18.4 × 26.7 cm); 8¾ × 13¾″ (22.2 × 34.9 cm); and 11¼ × 16″ (28.6 × 40.6 cm). For suppliers, refer to the source list at the back of this book. Or, you can make a simple substitute by following the directions below, which are for the smallest of the three standard-size screens.

MATERIALS

1 sheet of 7¼ × 10½″ (18.4 × 26.7 cm) black 10-ply poster board, cut into 4 panels measuring 7¼ × 2⅝″ (18.4 × 6.7 cm) each

1 sheet of plain gold gift wrap, slightly larger than 7¼ × 10½″ (18.4 × 26.7 cm)

Wax paper

Transparent tape

Black plastic tape ¾″ (1.91 cm) wide

Spray adhesive or water-soluble white glue

Scissors

Completed paper-cut in four sections (see design opposite)

PROCEDURE

1. Place the four poster-board panels side by side (Figure 1), leaving a slight space between each of them. (Otherwise the tape will pull loose when the screen is folded.) Make sure that the panels are evenly aligned along the top and down the sides.

FIGURE 1

2. Using transparent tape, attach the four panels to one another down the full length of each. Press the tape firmly into place.
3. Turn the panels over and attach them to one another on this side with black plastic tape down the length of each.
4. *Gently* fold each panel into position (Figure 2). Make certain that all your tape is holding. If any is loose, press it back firmly into place.

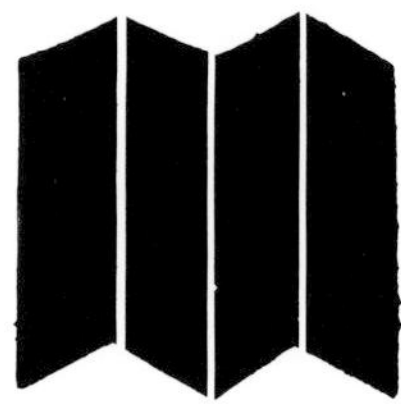

FIGURE 2

5. Straighten the taped panels out flat once again, and place them, the transparent tape side up, on a piece of wax paper.
6. Beginning at the right side, spray the first panel with adhesive (or cover it with water-soluble white glue). Align the right edge of your gold paper

with the right edge of the first panel, and smooth the gold paper into place, covering the first panel.
7. Spray or glue the second panel, and smooth the gold paper over it. Before the glue sets, fold the first panel over the second. This must be done to allow the paper to adjust to the fold. Flatten the panels out once again, and smooth any

Design for miniature screen, based on a traditional Chinese design.

folds or wrinkles in the gold paper.

8. Spray or glue the third panel; smooth the gold paper over it; then press this panel down on top of the fourth panel to allow the paper to adjust. Smooth out any folds or wrinkles.

9. Spray or glue the fourth panel; cover it with gold paper; then fold panels three and four together to adjust the paper. Smooth out any folds or wrinkles.

10. Trim any excess gold paper from around the edges of the screen.

11. Place the screen gold side up on a clean work surface. With the black plastic tape, make a frame ¼″ (0.64 cm) wide around the four edges of the screen. Fold the remainder of the tape over to the back to form a frame around that side.

12. Carefully and gently push the screen into a folded position (Figure 2).

13. Flatten the screen out once again, and apply your paper-cut to the four panels. *Note*: Your paper-cut must be in four sections; it will tear if you apply it in one piece and then try to fold it.

Cards

Paper-cuts adapt beautifully to note cards you can use for almost any occasion — birthdays, Christmas, Valentine's Day, and so on — depending on the design you create. And they're so easy to make!

Method One

MATERIALS

Sheet of good-quality paper for each card such as bond typewriter paper, available in white and a wide variety of colors

Completed paper-cut

Spray adhesive, rubber cement, or water-soluble white glue

PROCEDURE

1. Fold your paper in half (Figure 1).
2. Fold your paper over (Figure 2).
3. Glue your paper-cut in place on the front of the card (Figure 3).

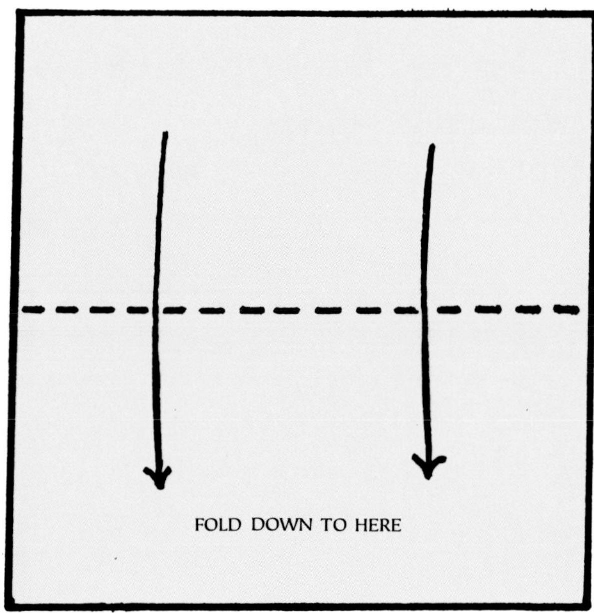

FIGURE 1

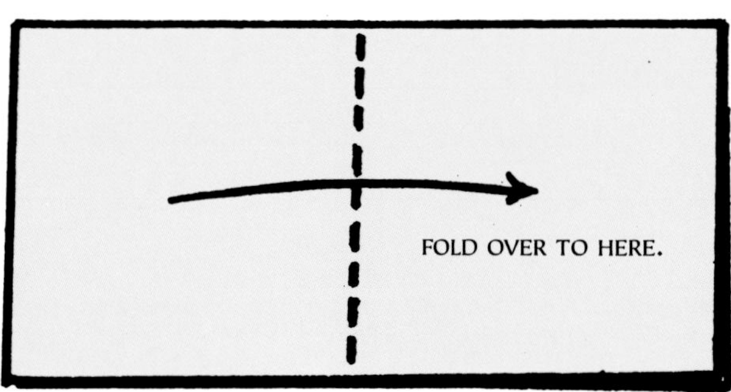

FIGURE 2

Christmas card.

FIGURE 3

Method Two

With this method you make the cut in the card itself, then back it with colored paper.

MATERIALS

Sheet of good-quality paper for each card

Pattern for the paper-cut you will make on the card

Sheet of colored paper the same size as your pattern, to serve as a background for your cut

Transparent tape or masking tape

X-Acto knife

Rubber cement or water-soluble white glue

PROCEDURE

1. Fold your paper according to steps 1 and 2 of method 1.

2. Unfold the paper and place it on your cutting surface.

3. Carefully tape your pattern onto the lower right-hand corner of the paper (Figure 4).

4. Cut out your paper-cut as you did for monochrome cuts.

5. Remove your pattern carefully so the tape does not tear the paper.

6. Apply rubber cement or water-soluble white glue to the back of your cut. Mount the cut on the colored paper.

7. Fold your paper back into a card.

FIGURE 4

Design for the Christmas card shown opposite.

SUNSET ON THE OLD RIVER.

A Final Note

IF YOU HAVE FOLLOWED these projects through step-by-step, you now have a large collection of artwork that I hope has given you much satisfaction and pleasure. I also hope that the techniques explained here have expanded your creativity and given you the impetus to create many more paper-cuts of your own design.

Next to collecting stamps, collecting paper-cuts is the fastest-growing hobby in the United States. Who knows — maybe your cuts will become choice additions to someone's prize collection. Happy cutting!

Cut-Art Supplies

AIKO'S ART MATERIALS IMPORT
714 N. Wabash Avenue
Chicago, IL 60611
Complete line of Japanese art supplies, including brushes, watercolors, sumi-e *and origami paper,* shikishi, *and* tanzaku. *Write for catalog.*

ARTHUR BROWN & BRO., INC.
2 W. 46th Street
New York, NY 10036
Complete line of art and paper supplies.

BACK STREET DESIGNS, INC.
P.O. Box 1213
Athens, AL 36511
Scherenschnitte *paper and pattern books.*

BROOKSTONE COMPANY
127 Vose Farm Road
Peterborough, NH 03458
Cutting bases, tweezers, surgical scalpels and blades, scissors. Write for catalog.

CHINA BOOKS AND PERIODICALS, INC.
Mail Order Department
2929—24th Street
San Francisco, CA 94110
Chinese paper-cuts and books on Chinese arts and crafts.

THE CRAFT BASKET
Colchester, CT 06415
Plastic tableware to decorate.

CROSS CREEK
4114 Lakeside Drive
Richmond, CA 94806
Scherenschnitte *paper and pattern books.*

DANIEL SMITH, INC.
4130 First Avenue S.
Seattle, WA 98134
Complete selection of art supplies, including handmade Japanese and other specialty papers.

DICK BLICK CO.
P.O. Box 1267
Galesburg, IL 61401;
P.O. Box 26
Allentown, PA 18105;
P.O. Box 521
Henderson, NV 89015;
1117 Alpharetta
Roswell, GA 30075
Mail-order art supplies and books.

DOVER PUBLICATIONS, INC.
31 E. 2d Street
Mineola, NY 11501
Extensive list of books on Japanese and Chinese designs, many of them copyright-free. Write for Fine Arts catalog.

FIDELITY PRODUCTS CO.
5601 International Parkway
P.O. Box 155
Minneapolis, MN 55440-0155
Write for Graphic Arts catalog.

JAPANPAPIER IMPORT GESELLSCHAFT
Drissler & Company
Postfach 930180
D-6000 Frankfurt am Main 93
Germany
Japanese paper.

JERRY'S ARTARAMA
P.O. Box 1105
New Hyde Park, NY 11040
Mail-order art supplies and books.

MITSUKOSHI LTD.
Foreign Department
Muromachi, Nihombashi, Chuo-ku
Tokyo, Japan
Complete line of Japanese art supplies.

PORTERS CAMERA STORE, INC.
P.O. Box 628
Cedar Falls, IA 50613
Two-piece plastic mugs to decorate.

RONIN GALLERY
605 Madison Avenue
New York, NY 10022
Wood-block prints and books on Japanese art.

TAKASHIMAYA CO., LTD.
General Information Office
4–1, Nihombashi-tori, 2-chome
Chuo-ku, Tokyo, Japan
Complete line of Japanese art supplies.

20TH CENTURY PLASTICS, INC.
3628 Crenshaw Boulevard
Los Angeles, CA 90051
Pressure-sensitive clear plastic film for laminating; acetate folders.

UCHIDA ART CO., LTD.
Mail Order Department
Kyoto Handicraft Center
Kumano Jinja Higashi, Sakyo-ku
Kyoto, 606 Japan
Miniature Japanese screens. Send for Wood-block Print Catalog.

Credits

Most of the works included in this book were conceived and executed by the author or are in his private collection. He gratefully acknowledges the following sources for the designs that appear on the pages noted below:

p. 11: from Feng-Kao Chang, "The Art of the Papercut," *China Reconstructs* 22, no. 12 (Beijing, 1973); p. 12, center: from W. M. Hawley, *Chinese Folk Design* (New York: Dover Publications, 1949); p. 12, bottom: adapted from Sergei Obraztsov, *The Chinese Puppet Theatre* (Boston: Plays Inc., 1961); p. 13: from Fumie Adachi (tr.), *Japanese Design Motifs* (New York: Dover Publications, 1972); p. 14, top: from Soētsu Yanagi, *Folk-Crafts in Japan* (Tokyo: Kokusai Bunka Shinkokai, 1936); p. 15: from Andrew W. Tuer, *Japanese Stencil Designs* (New York: Dover Publications, 1967); p. 17, bottom: from *Chinese Literature* 8 (Beijing, 1973); p. 30: adapted from Hajime Ōuichi, *Japanese Optical and Geometrical Art* (New York: Dover Publications, 1977); ancient *mon* motifs, p. 36; practice designs, bottom p. 47; and candleholder design, p. 148 (adaptation): from Robert Sietsema (comp.), *Oriental Designs* (New York: Hart Publishing, 1978); p. 40 and p. 42, top left: reproduced from *China Pictorial* (Beijing); p. 43: reproduced from *The Mucha Poster Coloring Book* (New York: Dover Publications, 1977); pp. 64, 68, 69: adapted from several designs in Theodore Menten (ed.), *Chinese Cut-Paper Designs* (New York: Dover Publications, 1975); p. 94: adapted from *Full-Color Designs from Chinese Opera Costumes* (New York: Dover Publications, 1980); pp. 96, 102, and front jacket: adapted from designs in Ed Hibbert, Jr., *Japanese Prints Coloring Book* (New York: Dover Publications, 1949); p. 130: adapted from *A Coloring Book of Japan* (San Francisco: Bellerophon Books, 1971) and J. Hillier, *Hokusai: Paintings, Drawings, and Woodcuts* (New York: E. P. Dutton, 1955); p. 132: adapted from an illustration by Katharine Sturges in Olive Beaupré Miller (ed.), *Little Pictures of Japan* (Chicago: The Book House for Children, 1925).

Select Bibliography

Adachi, Fumie, tr. *Japanese Design Motifs.* New York: Dover Publications, 1972.

Bendell, Ruth. *Paper Snipping Designs: The Silhouette Book.* Hinsdale, Ill.: Tree Toys, 1979.

Boyce, Charles W. "Paper." *The Encyclopedia Americana,* vol. 21. New York: Americana Corp., 1954.

Chang, Feng-Kao. "The Art of the Paper-cut." *China Reconstructs* 22, no. 12 (1973).

Christy, Anita. "Paper: Making and Mounting a Chinese Scroll." *Focus on Asian Studies* 2, no. 3 (1983).

D'Addetta, Joseph. *Treasury of Chinese Design Motifs.* New York: Dover Publications, 1981.

Day, JoAnne C. *Decorative Silhouettes of the Twenties for Designers and Craftsmen.* New York: Dover Publications, 1975.

Feng, Giang, ed. *Yan'an Papercuts.* Beijing: People's Fine Arts Publishing House, n.d.

Grafton, Carol Belanger, ed. *Silhouettes: A Pictorial Archive of Varied Illustrations.* New York: Dover Publications, 1979.

———. *More Silhouettes.* New York: Dover Publications, 1982.

"Hailun Paper-cuts." *China Pictorial* no. 7 (1979).

Hart, Harold H., comp. *The Illustrator's Handbook.* New York: A & W Visual Library, 1978.

Hawley, W. M. *Chinese Folk Design.* New York: Dover Publications, 1949.

———. *Japanese Crest Designs.* Hollywood, Calif.: W. M. Hawley, 1953.

Hibbert, Ed, Jr. *Japanese Prints Coloring Book.* New York: Dover Publications, 1982.

Honda, Isao. *Mon-kiri.* Tokyo: Japan Publications, 1972.

Jackson, Mrs. E. Nevill. *Silhouettes: A History and Dictionary of Artists.* New York: Dover Publications, 1981.

Lehner, Ernst. *Symbols, Signs, and Signets.* New York: Dover Publications, 1950.

Lichten, Frances. *Folk Art Motifs of Pennsylvania.* New York: Charles Scribner's Sons, 1946.

Melchers, Bernd, ed. *Traditional Chinese Paper-cut Designs.* New York: Dover Publications, 1978.

Menten, Theodore, ed. *Chinese Cut-paper Designs.* New York: Dover Publications, 1975.

Miyata, Masayuki. *Genshoku Kiri-e Ga-Shū.* Tokyo: Kodansha, 1972. (In Japanese.)

———. *Kiri-e Ga-Shū.* Tokyo: Kodansha, 1973. (In Japanese.)

Nippon Kiri-e Kyokai. *Kiri-e.* Japan: Shufu-to-Seikatsusha, 1980. (In Japanese.)

Obraztsov, Sergei. *The Chinese Puppet Theatre,* tr. J. T. MacDermott. Boston: Plays Inc., 1961.

Ōuchi, Hajime. *Japanese Optical and Geometrical Art.* New York: Dover Publications, 1977.

"Papercuts: A Chinese Art." *Chinatown Souvenir Book.* Los Angeles: Chinese Chamber of Commerce, 1973.

"Puppets Still Cast a Big Shadow." *Free China Weekly* 22, no. 37 (1981).

Sietsema, Robert, comp. *Oriental Designs.* New York: Hart Publishing, 1978.

Stalberg, Roberta Helmer, and Ruth Nesi. *China's Crafts: The Story of How They're Made and What They Mean.* New York: China Books and Periodicals/ Eurasia Press, 1980.

Sze, Mai-Mai. *The Way of Chinese Painting.* New York: Vintage Books, 1959.

Tang, Chi-shiang. "Foshan Scissor-Cuts." *Chinese Literature* 8 (1973).

Temko, Florence. *Chinese Paper Cuts: Their Story and How to Make and Use Them.* San Francisco: China Books and Periodicals, 1982.

———. *Folk Crafts for World Friendship.* Garden City, N.Y.: Doubleday and UNICEF, 1976.

Temko, Florence, and Toshie Takahama. *The Magic of Kirigama: Happenings with Paper and Scissors.* Tokyo: Japan Publications, 1978.

Tuer, Andrew W. *Japanese Stencil Designs.* New York: Dover Publications, 1967.

Warner, John. *Chinese Papercuts.* Hong Kong: John Warner Publications, 1978.

Williams, C. A. S. *Outlines of Chinese Symbolism and Art Motives.* Shanghai: Kelly & Walsh, 1941.

"The World of Kiri-e." *Japan* 11, no. 3 (1973).

Yanagi, Sōetsu. *Folk-crafts in Japan.* Tokyo: Kokusai Bunka Shinkokai, 1936.

Index